Vietnam

Journey of Unexpected Delights

Susan Rogers

Published by Pip & Tinks Publishing

ISBN: 978-0-9928634-1-8

Other books in the Travelling Solo series

Brazil and Argentina: From Jungle to Icebergs

Dedicated to Jennie Bone, the English teacher who had faith in me.

ACKNOWLEDGMENTS

I am grateful to Chris Stewart and Kapka Kassabova for their excellent tuition and encouragement.
Many thanks to Ian and Annie for taking the time to read early drafts and to Jessica for the final proofing.
And thank you Aaron Hendricks (Aaronik Designs) for the front cover design.

Table of Contents

Introduction

This is a story adapted from a diary that I kept at the time, which aims to inspire single people to try participating in those events normally associated with couples, whether that it is going out for a meal alone, going to the cinema by yourself or in this case taking a solo holiday. It is also a travelogue of a fascinating journey through Vietnam.

At the time of visiting Vietnam in 2003 I was aged forty-something, with a demanding career and I was most definitely in need of a break. My ideal holiday is giving my brain a rest from the normal routine and exploring foreign cultures. I don't like beach holidays, partly because I hate getting sand into every crevice and finding it lurking in the corners of my suitcase three years later, and partly because I get bored if I chill out and do nothing more than read a book and sip the occasional beer. So I chose Vietnam because it promised to offer a totally different culture and a variety of interesting places to occupy my time.

Leading up to the trip I wasn't especially in "holiday mode." I had been very busy at work and instead of spending any of my spare time planning the break as I would normally do; I'd given a brief to a travel agent and asked them to sort something out for me.

A few days before the journey started, although I was excited at the prospect of getting away from work and visiting Vietnam for the first time, I was also feeling a little sad and somewhat apprehensive, as airports are always teeming with couples hugging and touching excitedly, looking forward to the holiday ahead. I was travelling

1

alone. I had been divorced for around fifteen years, and although I had had boyfriends since, I was single again.

It was true that I'd rather go on holiday by myself than not at all but I'd rather voyage with a "special" travel companion than without. I had taken solitary holidays before, however this was my first long haul vacation without a partner, and realising that there would almost certainly be emotional and practical obstacles to negotiate it made sense to join a tour group. I would be teaming up with the party when I arrived in Saigon and anticipated that there would be at least a few people I would like, be able to sit with at dinner and then hopefully keep in touch with after the holiday to reminisce with. I wouldn't be totally alone once I'd arrived in Vietnam.

This combination of apprehension and excitement heightened as the first day of the journey dawned.

The Start - 19th December

I sat up sharply in bed. It was pitch black and I didn't feel as if I'd been asleep. I glanced over to the alarm clock strategically positioned at the other side of the room so that I had to physically get out of bed to turn it off. It was 5.30am and since the alarm was due to go off at 6.00am anyway, I thought I might as well get up. I am a naturally early riser, however the village where I lived had been prone to power cuts at the time and I definitely didn't want to sleep in that day. The alarm was set to the "extremely piercing" setting because on those rare occasions when its use was imperative, I was only one step away from comatose.

I started running the bath, padded downstairs to make a coffee, and was then suddenly plunged into darkness. Goddamnit! I fumbled around for a lighter and gingerly made my way to the kitchen and the bowl of ever-ready candles. I glued three to a side plate with their own molten wax and carried on as normal. I smiled to myself. It was potentially good training for a holiday in Vietnam, a country known to have had an erratic electricity grid. I finished packing the last few items and left the house by candlelight. As I was about to drive away the electricity returned and the house looked like The Blackpool Illuminations due to all of the rooms where I hadn't turned off the lights. Dazzling bright lights from every orifice were made even more intense by the lack of any other light pollution. Oh bugger. I only had my car key with me as the rest of the bunch was secreted away to minimise surplus to requirements stuff I was carrying. I needed to find the first hidden key which led to the second that would open Fort Knox.

3

With the lights extinguished, keys re-hidden and normality restored, I drove away.

Terminal 3 was its usual nightmare with numerous people having no concept of invading the personal space of others, and was just generally crowded, dirty, and noisy.

I spied the snake-like queue for Economy check in. There must have been a hundred people at least, and I then admittedly had a sense of relief and smugness as I was travelling business class where there were only four queuing travellers. I hadn't paid for business class, but had used the many years of accumulated air miles that were about to expire to upgrade the flight. It was a case of use them or lose them, and of course there would be advantages. Skipping a long queue was most definitely an advantage.

I moved seamlessly through into the crowded departure lounge. Far too small a space for far too many people. I did the obligatory round of duty free shops buying nothing, and then felt decidedly hungry. I realised that I hadn't eaten a proper meal for a few days what with all the pre-holiday rushing about, and so I decided to start off the vacation with a "full English". The only place I could get one was O'Neils bar. As I made my order I noticed that not only was I surrounded by Guinness swilling travellers, but I was the only person ordering solid food for breakfast. It was 8.30am. My order was simple.

"Full breakfast with a round of dry bread please." The full breakfast was the easy part.

"Dry bread?"

4

"Yes please. Bread without any butter or spread."

"We don't have dry bread" said the heavily made up girl behind the counter "we only have

Toast."

"But surely, if you offer toast you could also give me a slice of bread?"

"Sorry. No bread. Just toast."

I asked in a somewhat bemused manner whether it was possible to order un-toasted toast? She beamed at me.

"Yes I guess that's possible." So I ordered a full English breakfast with un-toasted toast, no butter. The order arrived, and I got exactly what I wanted.

Stoked up, I extricated myself from the mayhem of the main terminal and relaxed in the tranquillity of the Malaysian Airlines Business Lounge. It was a lovely lounge – spacious and clean, with the gentle sound of trickling fountains and soft relaxing muzak.

As boarding time was fast approaching, I had one last opportunity for a quick cigarette. I headed towards the smoking room and instantly felt as if I'd slipped into a scene from Metropolis, the dark and foreboding German silent science fiction film set in a futuristic grey urban dystopia. The room was large, cavernous, dark, murky and smoky with people sitting quietly along the sides of the room as though they were zombies frozen in time. A truly disgusting place, it was almost enough to provoke instant quitting, but not quite. I had a cigarette that I didn't really want, but I was conscious that the next opportunity would be in thirteen plus hours.

Joe had sent me a text wishing me a good holiday. Joe had been my partner for four years and we not only split amicably, but remained best friends even though he had another partner now. For years I had considered him the brother I never had. I gave him a quick call.

"What a coincidence," he said. "I've literally just opened an atlas to look up Vietnam, as I hadn't a clue where it was other than somewhere in Asia." There was a brief pause.

"I've found it!" he exclaimed and then asked excitedly,

"Are you going to see Saigon?"

"Yes, that's where I'm flying to today, although it's now called Ho Chi Minh City," I replied.

"I've heard of Saigon," he announced proudly, "that's where The King and I comes from."

"No," I said with a smile, "that was Siam."

"Oh" he said a little disappointedly, but then perked up with, "Is Siam in Vietnam?"

"No. Siam is now called Thailand." I loved Joe to bits.

It was time to board, and I handed over my boarding pass only for the screen to tell the operator that I'd already boarded. Oh no, surely not an argument over seats before the holiday had even started? On the contrary, I had been randomly selected for an upgrade to First Class. Nice start!

The flight was long. Twelve hours to Kuala Lumpur. The choice of in-flight videos wasn't that great but I watched a couple that were reasonably entertaining; "Pirates of the Caribbean" a relatively new release, and "Matchstick Men".

First Class Malaysian seating may not have been as comfortable as British Airways Business Class, but the food was the best I'd ever had on any airline. Dinner alone was too many courses to count – satay, hors d'ouvres, caviar, soup, beef vindaloo, cheese, fruit and sweets. Breakfast was similarly extravagant. By the time we were approaching Kuala Lumpur I was already feeling enormous and extremely appreciative of the extra wide seating. Another advantage to having been upgraded. How fortuitous that I was wearing elasticated slacks for a comfortable journey.

There were some pangs of nostalgia as I strolled through Kuala Lumpur airport. The last time I had been here was with Joe following the disastrous Malaysian holiday. It hadn't been the beginning of the end of the relationship, but the end of the end. I didn't feel pangs for Joe, but it highlighted the fact that now I was travelling alone. I had a lump in my throat and could feel my eyes glistening. *No Susan – you have to keep control* I had thought to myself. I had told everyone that I'd rather have a holiday alone than miss out, and this was true, but they generally underestimated just how much courage and resilience it took to do this. Sightseeing by myself with no one to discuss the places of interest. Eating on my own with nobody to laugh about the highlights of the day. Drinking alone and retiring early so that you didn't look as if you were hanging around bars waiting to be picked up. At least I would be meeting the other group members on my arrival in Saigon, and that cheered my spirits...

The wait at Kuala Lumpur airport was only an hour, so I had just enough time to go to the Executive Lounge, freshen up, wash my malaria tablet down with a strong coffee and then head for the connecting flight to Ho Chi Minh City........

Saigon - 20th December

I was first off the plane, first through immigration and first outside. There were huge crowds of people waiting in arrivals. However, it was not as busy an airport as one might have thought at first, as I was told later that when someone returns to the country, the whole family comes out to greet them. Literally aunties, uncles, grandparents, siblings, nieces and nephews.

I needed to find a person holding a "Destination Asia" board but there was nobody in sight. I asked a few of the other reps gathering in their sheep. No, they didn't know where I'd find one either. It was hot and sticky, and I was decidedly tired. After a relatively easy journey the last thing I wanted was to be stranded at Ho Chi Minh airport. I didn't even know which hotel I was staying at as the rep would have my vouchers, so it was pointless grabbing a taxi and heading off under my own steam.

I did the round of boards a couple more times then just as I was about to phone the Destination Asia 24 hours help-line, I spotted a little man with a board that had my name on it. He shook my hand firmly and introduced himself as Jung, then phoned his driver to come and collect us. I thought it was a rather nice touch having a driver to take me personally to the hotel, but then it was probably the more practical option if the other tourists were arriving on different flights. I pondered that there may even be time to shower and change before meeting up with the rest of the group later. The car pulled up and Jung held the door open for me as the driver loaded my suitcase.

"Are you going to be my tour guide?" I asked Jung.

"Yes," he replied, "for the southern area, and then you'll have a different guide for the other parts of your holiday." I was impressed by his impeccable English. He was immaculately dressed in a smart black suit, fresh white shirt and a dark corporate tie. His shiny jet black hair looked freshly trimmed, washed and combed so that not a single tuft was out of place. He wore a genuine beaming smile and a friendly expression that fanned up to his eyes and beyond.

"How many people will we have in the tour group?" I queried. Jung looked at me as if I'd just landed from a distant planet.

"One," he said. "You." Whilst I was still in shock he went on to explain that Destination Asia prefer to organize their trips in small groups or couples because then you have your personal guide, you can change the itinerary to suit, go off the beaten track and so on. I was extremely shaken by this news, and it tipped me out of my comfort zone with a bump as I had been assuming all along that I'd be joining a group once I got to Vietnam. I slumped back into the taxi seat and sized it all up.

There were definitely very mixed feelings about being the only person. I had expected to have other people to talk to, other people to dine with, and other people to share the holiday experience with, both during the holiday and then hopefully afterwards keep in touch and re-live some of the highlights that would inevitably happen. I wouldn't have the security and solace of others. Would I cope? Would I survive the duration? Would I be so miserable that it would spoil the holiday? On the other hand though, this promised to be a very different holiday from the average, I'd probably get to see more of the authentic Vietnam rather than just the carefully selected tourist points of interest, and meet locals instead of tourists. The question was, did I have the confidence to believe in my independence, or would I be driven crazy with isolation?

If nothing else, it would certainly prove to be a character-forming holiday. Could I cope with my own company for a fortnight? Could I turn those *what if's* into *why not's*? What about that solitary dining table in the corner of restaurants that I'm inevitably given so that I didn't spoil the symmetry? Well, I managed to do it on business travel, so why not on holiday. I guess I'd know one way or the other in two weeks' time. No, I wasn't going to let the fact that I was not only travelling solo, but also now travelling alone to spoil the holiday. I was primarily here to explore the culture and diversity of Vietnam, not to make a new bunch of friends, so I sat up, looked out of the window, and started to absorb the scenes outside.

My first impression of Ho Chi Minh City was a cross between Malaysia and China. On the surface it seemed fairly modern, certainly for an Asian country judging by the quality of the road system. But upon looking more carefully, the buildings were old and crumbling, and there were old men squatting by the side of the road as only Asians seem to be able to do without toppling over, playing a Vietnamese version of draughts. Many women were wearing coolie hats and carrying onerous amounts of goods in swing baskets which were balanced on yokes over their shoulders. There were motor bikes and cycle rickshaws everywhere. It was most definitely a very lively and bustling city.

11

Motorbikes and bicycles were parked randomly on the pavements and overhead was a spaghetti of electric cables feeding the shop fronts and the houses down deep alleyways. There would be a row of relatively new concrete but peeling buildings, then suddenly a bright and colourful little Chinese house slotted incongruently between them. Their roofs had wave-like green ceramic tiles suggesting that they were regular dwellings rather than palaces or temples which would have been gold or red. When it came to buildings, the Chinese placed more emphasis on width than height which was another reason why they looked so squat and cartoon like wedged between their modern neighbours. The buildings had several pitched roofs with decorated gables, all displaying the sweeping curvature that rises at the corners, that graceful upward slope so typical of old oriental architecture, the eaves overhanging the stout load bearing wooden timbers. The roofs' apexes were decorated with a range of creatures, objects and symbols to bring good health and happiness to the family that dwelled within and the heavy flaking wooden doors bore talismen and imagery for good fortune.

Occasionally a comical sight would whiz past the car, such as a small moped carrying two people, one sitting on the prescribed seat and the other perched on the petrol tank, with a huge basket precariously fixed to the back containing half a dozen squawking chickens. Or a cycle rickshaw burdened under the weight of a three piece suite wobbling on the makeshift stretcher strapped by all too few ropes to the main frame of the vehicle.

The New World Hotel was alleged to be the best in Ho Chi Minh City, but also in the whole of Vietnam. It was however the same as any business hotel I had stayed at anywhere in the world and possessed no special ambience at all. What a shame as I would have preferred an old colonial type place with character or something more typically Vietnamese. Still, I didn't plan to be spending much time in the hotel, as I wanted to be out and about exploring. Anyway, a lesson learned for future holidays, write a more detailed holiday brief and pay extra attention to the booking details.

I checked in and decided to exchange some money. I became an instant millionaire. There were approximately 27,000 Dong to the Pound. I changed £60 and receive over £1.6 million Dong. It was going to be very difficult working out the number of zeros on each bank note. I might accidentally tip someone 50,000 Dong instead of 5,000. Then again, the former was less than two quid. The worst mistake I could possibly make would be with their largest note, 100,000 Dong, but as that was less than £4, I was unlikely to bankrupt myself during the holiday through error.

It was now early afternoon, and Jung was leaving me for the day. He told me that it was very safe out on the streets if I wanted to go exploring, and the only thing I had to be careful of was the traffic and crossing the roads. He advised me to take the same "security" care that I would anywhere in the world, but pick-pocketing was minimal and bodily attacks very rare. It was a safe place to be. They had very strict punishments for crimes - drug handling merited the death penalty as did other major crimes and there were long jail sentences for theft and such like.

I freshened up and went down to the reception to see if they had a telephone directory. Stephen, a musician friend and writer back home, had asked if I would look up an old friend of his named Rupert, a reporter based out here, but as he hadn't heard from him for around twenty years the chances of me finding him were extremely slim. It would however be good fun to meet up with a total stranger, in an unusual location, and especially someone who would know the country inside out. With fingers crossed I asked at the reception. Unfortunately residential telephone directories did not exist, only business Yellow Pages. I asked how people found phone numbers. There was a directory enquiries service, but you had to have a name and an address. I only had a name. I asked her if she would at least try directory enquiries, as looking for an unusual English name they may not need an address. I wrote his name in large letters on a piece of paper and smiled very persuasively at her. She made the call and spoke to someone in Vietnamese, but they wouldn't check a name without an address. I thanked her for at least trying.

I found the business centre in the hotel where I could access my e-mails so I searched for the British Embassy in Saigon and sent them an e-mail asking if they could help me track down someone while I was visiting. I didn't hold out much hope, but it was worth a try.

Not wanting to waste any more time at the hotel and desiring to explore my surroundings, I stepped out into the streets of Ho Chi

Minh City. Crossing the road was a most interesting experience. The traffic was mainly motorbikes, with the occasional car, bus, lorry, rickshaw, and bicycle. The roads were quite wide and there were bikers riding about 7 abreast - in each direction, so Jung had certainly been wise to warn me about taking care.

I came across a huge indoor market buzzing with activity. The cavernous hall was divided into sections, and within these main sections there were further subdivisions with passageways barely one person wide running between the stalls. Each section was dedicated to one particular trade, so there were about 20 clothes stalls, 20 footwear stalls, 20 sweet stalls etc. The locals were sitting or squatting by their stalls eating noodles or soup. I suddenly felt like I was in the land of pygmies when I realised that I was a good head and shoulders above the Vietnamese - including the men, and I'm not especially tall. Everyone looked at me, most of them smiled and I smiled back, but as the only European walking around their market I wondered who the tourist attraction was here. I'd have liked to have taken some photos, but I wasn't sure of the local protocol yet and I didn't want to offend if it wasn't appropriate. In any case, I knew that once I had a feel for the country and the culture, there would be plenty more opportunities.

As I walked around, my nostrils were invaded with the powerful aroma of Oriental spices. Warm heavily pungent cumin; the liquorice odour of fennel; the sweet smell of cloves; the sharp zing of ginger root and the tangy citrus smell of lemongrass. With my nose gently tingling, I walked back onto the street and made my way to a road that Jung had pointed out to me on the way to the hotel, where there were shops selling cheap DVDs and CDs.

The shops didn't have glass frontages but opened straight onto the street, with metal blinds that they would pull down and lock at night. In one shop, a guy was sitting at his computer, blatantly copying CDs for the whole world to see and I realised that "cheap" actually meant "pirated." I flicked through some DVDs but was not sure whether they would be in English, and in any case, none of them jumped out at me to be added to my collection. I was then drawn to the computer software section where two CDs caught my eye. One was software for easily creating a web site which I'd been thinking of buying for a while and the other was the full version of some music writing software, the same one that I used back home but only the limited function freebie download version. I asked how much the software disks were. They were 8,000 Dong each. About twenty five pence. As the software cost about £95 in the UK I was extremely tempted, however I'd heard of horror stories of viruses corrupting computers to the point of destruction because of dodgy software and I just wasn't prepared to take the risk, so I smiled at the chap, shook my head and moved on.

It was time to head back to the hotel. It was quite dusty and not only were the bikers wearing protective facemasks but many of the pedestrians were too. In the gutter I passed a clump of incense sticks burning for no apparent reason. There was neither a little shrine, nor any people sitting around, it merely stood alone, its bright fuchsia and yellow sticks a contrast to the grey dusty pavement. There were some pretty mephitic sewers nearby but I doubted that the incense would have made that much difference. I must hasten to add, that there were only a few smelly spots as generally speaking, the streets and roads were clean of waste and debris, and I felt extremely positive about my first venture out onto the streets.

There was still daylight so I decided to relax by the hotel pool for a while and instantly fell asleep. When I awoke, I began reading a novel called Accordion Crimes and judging by the first couple of chapters it promised to be a good read. It was the story of an accordion that was passed or sold from person to person, with each new owner playing a different genre of music. I had recently taken up playing the instrument again after a lapse of nearly thirty years, and had my first ever tuition a matter of a few weeks before I came away, having previously been self taught. I had learned in the first lesson that I hadn't even been holding the accordion correctly for all that time. As the sun set, it became a little too cool to stay by the pool, so I returned to the hotel room, where I lay down on the bed for a few minutes, fell asleep and then awoke again at around 7.30pm. I couldn't decide whether to go to bed and recover from the flight or go and have some dinner. I decided on the latter, otherwise I'd wake in the middle of the night with the munchies, and I hadn't packed any chocolate bars.

Although it was an international business hotel and therefore the buffet was pretty much what you'd expect anywhere in the world, with numerous platters of salad and local meats, the detailed composition of such buffets was always an adventure and exploration in its own right. It was one of those days when I wished I ate oysters and raw fish, because the display and selection available was absolutely stunning. The salad bar offered dishes based on bamboo shoots, water chestnuts, fennel, bean sprouts and other vegetables I didn't recognise, but most fascinating was the soup bar. They had three pots of simmering stock (beef, chicken and vegetable) and dishes upon dishes of potential additions. The attendant didn't speak any English at all so I pointed to the raw chicken pieces and several of the vegetables. She added these to a strainer and dropped it into the appropriate pot of stock. The broth was brought to my table and it was one of the most delicious soups I had ever tasted.

Being alone, it was my "classic" hotel meal, something that I had perfected over the last couple of years when travelling solo for business. Eat slowly, down a couple of local beers, write some diary notes and read my book. By pausing suitably between the various courses I could manage to make dinner stretch to an hour and a half.

I also reflected that my expectations had been that I would now be sitting down at a large table with strangers from the tour, swapping travel stores and generally getting to know each other. Was I missing it? No I actually wasn't, but that could have been because I was very tired and the effort of polite conversation wouldn't have come easily. I smiled to myself in recognition of surviving the first day and not even noticing the absence of others.

It was only just after 9.00pm when I retired, but I was so shattered that I fell into bed and to sleep immediately. However, I was awake at 3.00am. Wide-awake just as I was before I left home so many hours ago. I couldn't get back to sleep so turned on the television to see if there was anything to watch. HBO had just started showing Forrest Gump, one of my favourites so I watched it expecting to slowly drift off, but I didn't go back to sleep.

Cu Chi Tunnels - 21st December

Breakfast was buffet style with an excellent selection on offer. Especially tasty were the huge crunchy but juicy grapefruits called pomela. It was the first time I'd eaten them, indeed the first time I had even heard of them and I went back for seconds. Sitting close by, certainly within hearing distance were a couple of "know-it-all" Brits lecturing others on the adjacent table as to what they should go and see. They spoke as if from detailed firsthand knowledge, but it became evident pretty quickly that they were basically regurgitating a guide book and some of the places they had yet to visit themselves.

"I assume you are going to visit the Mekong Delta," bellowed the paunchy man in his ridiculously out of place cravat.

"Yes, we are hoping to," replied the timid honeymooners.

"Well take it from me that it is definitely worth getting up very early to visit the floating market," Mr Bombastic continued, "and take plenty of mozzie repellent. The little buggers can eat you raw."

"Thanks, we'll remember that," they nervously commented. "What time of the year did you visit? We've heard they can be worse in some months."

"Erm" said Mr Bombastic a little flustered, his jowls turning cherry pink "I haven't been there yet, but I was in Panama last year so I'm assuming it's similar."

I prepared the camera bag and day bag before heading down to reception for my 8.30am pickup. I had three cameras with me, a little over the top I know, but there was method in my madness. A newly purchased digital point and shoot so that I would have lots of instant photos to look at back home, my trusty old friend the 35mm Samsung with exceptionally good quality photos especially for those scenic shots that required such a camera to capture their majesty, and a Sony camcorder for movies. My day bag, as I've always called my small black back pack, carried the essentials for the day. A packet of wet ones because I hate having sticky fingers, bottled water, paper tissues, a small medical pack, purse, notepad, pen, cigarettes, lighter and penknife. It also contained a wedge of biro pens on this occasion, the reason for which will become apparent later.

Jung arrived spot on 8.30, delighted that I was ready and waiting. We were heading to the Cu Chi area which was especially renowned for its tunnels and Jung took the opportunity en-route to give me some historical background and explain other interesting facts.

"Jung, yesterday afternoon when I went out for a walk I noticed that many of the female bikers were wearing long gloves up to their elbows, and facemasks. Is this due to dust and pollution or just the latest fashion?" I quizzed.

"I guess it's sort of related to fashion as it's to keep them white. The paler they are, the more beautiful they perceive themselves to be. The rich people even pay a lot of money for special bleaching treatments to remain white. Hey, somewhat different to you

22

Europeans who lie in the sun determined to get dark skin, but usually ending up the colour of a London bus!" he answered laughing.

"Why do some people call the city Ho Chi Minh City, and others call it Saigon?" I continued.

"Well, the old, original quarters of the city are still called Saigon. The greater city area is Ho Chi Minh City. Saigon is effectively a district within Ho Chi Minh City, a little like Manhattan and New York."

Jung proudly announced that property prices with regard to land per square metre in Saigon and Hanoi were amongst the most expensive in the world, even more so than Singapore or Tokyo. Although this probably put property ownership out of reach for many, I could see from Jung's body language that he was extremely proud of his country having expensive housing as this equalled affluence and in turn meant 'developed country'. It was because of the cost of land that houses and shop frontages were exceptionally narrow and then people built up 3 or 4 stories. Somehow this fact about Saigon and Hanoi having such relatively expensive land didn't quite ring true for me, so I checked the facts when I returned home, and nowhere in Vietnam featured in the top twenty. Perhaps Jung meant the most expensive in Vietnam, and this I could believe because they were the two largest municipalities.

He also imparted some interesting facts about money. Virtually no Vietnamese people used banks and it was a cash economy as they just didn't trust them. As a result it was very difficult for the government to work out tax and only 600,000 people out of a population of 80 million paid tax. Those who saved, bought gold and hid it at home whilst some turned it into dollars. Jung showed me a small gold bar about the size and thickness of a credit card that he carried around in his wallet. He said he had more of them at home. Well hidden.

"Whenever I have saved up enough cash I go and buy more gold bars. You never know what is going to happen to currency these days, even dollars, but you can always depend on gold," he said

I asked Jung to tell me more about the last war as I was too young at the time to pay it much attention and my knowledge was based largely on movies, mainly American films such as The Deer Hunter, Platoon, We Were Soldiers and the like, although there were a few attempts to show a more rounded perspective, such as Casualties of War and Born on the Fourth of July.

I suspected that I would get a biased perspective during my visit to Vietnam, and it certainly wouldn't be the American bias, but if I kept my ears open throughout the holiday with my educational antennae primed, and asked similar questions of different people, by the end of the trip I would hopefully have sufficient facts to paint a broader picture.

"It's very sad," Jung started "but war has dominated years of Vietnam's history and although people think of the Vietnam War as being the fight between the Vietnamese communists called VietCong, and the Americans, the wars actually went back much further than that. The modern story starts with it becoming a French colony in the eighteen hundreds. The French treated the Vietnamese people appallingly and even many visiting Frenchmen today were horrified and stunned at the treatment imposed by their own countrymen. I had some French tourists last year and they cried at everything I showed them and told them. As a colony we had no rights and the French strictly enforced their own rule. It's therefore not really surprising at the time that the Vietnamese had a very bad first hand view of western democracy and why there was willingness and acceptance to follow the emerging communist leaders."

"I can well understand that" I interjected sympathetically, "Not exactly the right tactic to foster good relations". Jung continued.

"The struggle for independence that began with the communists fighting French colonial power in the 1940s did not end until the communists seized Saigon in 1954 and subsequently control of the whole country in 1975. The period that Americans refer to as the "Vietnam War", and that the Vietnamese call the "American War", was from 1965 to 1973."

"You certainly know your history," I added, urging him to tell me more.

"Ha! I studied at university for three years to become a tour guide. The exams were very hard. I had to learn so many facts and figures because it was drummed into us not only to know our own history in great depth, all the dates and such, but also to be prepared for unusual questions from tourists! I pride myself that so far I have been able to answer all questions!"

"Please, carry on with the history," I implored.

"At the start of this last war, the country was split into the communist north led by the nationalist leader Ho Chi Minh and the pro-American south with the two areas divided by a demilitarised zone. Country-wide elections to decide a permanent solution were promised but never happened and within five years the communists had launched a guerrilla war on the south. Hundreds of thousands of US soldiers were sent to help fight against the communists in a costly and ultimately unsuccessful war which brought domestic civil unrest and international embarrassment. What drove the Americans to pursue this futile war were their concerns about the spread of communism and the belief that if one nation fell to this ideology another would follow soon after and then another so it was better to nip it in the bud before it spread. We were the country they were nipping in the bud.

"In 1965, with the South Vietnamese army making little headway against the VietCong, the United States launched a sustained bombing campaign against targets in North Vietnam. It became clear pretty quickly that airpower alone was not going to give victory to the Americans and it was at that point that ground troops were deployed." I was fascinated by the history but Jung said that he would continue the story when we reached the tunnels, as it was a more suitable environment to tell me about the next phase.

The drive to the tunnels took a little over an hour so I sank back in my seat and watched the paddy fields and small plantations glide past.

The Cu Chi tunnels (within the Cu Chi area) are an extensive network of underground tunnels that span almost 125 miles. Jung said that a lot of people think they were built during the American Wars, but in fact they were first used by the Viet Minh (the nationalist soldiers who fought against the Japanese during World War Two) to hide from the French, and only later became hideouts for the VietCong, who used them for surprise attacks on the Americans. Interestingly, although the term VietCong was generally believed to mean "Vietnamese communists" in the western world, this was a misnomer as the correct name for the organisation was the National Liberation Front. Although the NLF was supported and trained by the northern communist government, many of its actual regular members were just peasant farmers with little, if any, in depth political awareness or knowledge. VietCong was effectively a slang term created by the Americans. Many VC lived underground for months even years, surviving on tapioca, and getting fresh air through an ingenious and elaborate ventilation system.

The tunnels started with individuals building their own personal "dug out" to hide from the French. When they were running short of food, they would burrow underground to join up with a neighbouring tunnel, a neighbour who hopefully would have some food or water. These gradually developed, until an underground city was built with central food and medical supplies, meeting rooms and later munitions supplies.

"Some of the tunnels were underneath one of the US military bases," quipped Jung, "and the VietCong would come out at night, raid the American camp for food and then disappear back into the tunnels. It took the Americans months to work out that they had set up camp right over such an underground network." He chuckled a little as he finished the sentence.

The tourist tour trails through woodland and I commented to Jung that it didn't look how I had imagined it to be. I'd always expected it to be tropical rainforest with swamps and giant leafy trees blocking out most of the sunlight. Apparently it was fifty years ago but the Americans blitzed over 80% of the forest and it had never grown back as it was. After bombing the land or spraying it with chemicals such as the toxic herbicide Agent Orange, the Americans dropped seed so that elephant grass grew. This had very thick, sharp foliage, impossible to walk through without ripping your skin to shreds, so that alone acted as a deterrent. Once this had been grown the Americans then burned it, the idea being that there would be several feet of ash, and therefore footprints of VietCong activity obviously visible as they seemed to move around invisibly.

"Agent Orange that was sprayed over the jungle to destroy the thick foliage that VietCong fighters used for cover also left a particularly nasty side effect," Jung said sombrely. "Many babies were still-born with awful defects, spinal problems or multiple limbs and hundreds of thousands of surviving children suffered severe life-long birth defects."

I couldn't say anything to this. If I told Jung how I felt, which was a total lack of understanding as to why or how a nation could inflict such pain and misery on so many innocent people, it would have sounded shallow and inadequate.

28

The Cu Chi tunnel area alone had 8 million tons of bombs dropped on it, 4 times more than the total of all bombs during the Second World War. So although there was now a forest, it was not of the same type that was there fifty plus years ago. Their rain forests had been decimated.

The first sign of the tunnels was a hidden entrance. A square hole in the ground covered with a wooden lid, which in turn was covered with leaves thus camouflaging it to the outside world. A person would slip into the hole with his arms above his head, and then pull the lid back over the hole, and it became invisible. The hole was so small that only a thin person would get in. Jung asked me if I wanted to climb into the hole to see what it was like, but knowing that I won't get my bum through I decided to avoid the embarrassment of even trying. I watched a couple of other people have a go. One was a man of beanpole stature and the other a young boy. There were lots of these entrance squares throughout the jungle. They had been carefully constructed in an internal triangular shape to minimize damage by a direct bomb attack. However, even past the very small entrance hole at the top of the triangle, the tunnels didn't get significantly larger.

I was shown a display of extremely nasty looking man traps devised and set by the VietCong. They all featured pointed bamboo sticks in some configuration or other and they all pretty much worked on the principle of a balanced board of some type, covered with leaves, then when pressure was applied in certain places the board would collapse impaling the victim on the spikes. Many of these were quite small contraptions and apparently were designed not to kill, but to injure. The VietCong reckoned that the more injured American soldiers there were, then the more healthy soldiers would be required to take care of them thereby reducing the fighting capacity of the American army. Although I initially thought that "designed not to kill" was undiluted propaganda, when I saw the contraptions they did indeed look as if they were designed for small nasty injuries rather than instant death. There and again, they may have been designed for painful slow death rather than a quick instant death. I decided to keep an open mind.

One particularly nasty device was called the 'Saigon Souvenir'. This was a cage about the size of a lobster pot, with bamboo or metal spikes around the edges and a large upward facing barb in the middle. The victim of such a contraption would get a 12-inch spike through the bottom of their foot, and about 8 spikes in the leg. The only way of extracting such a victim would be to dig out the cage, still attached to the leg of the victim, and remove it later, or amputate the leg there and then for a quick escape. Again, allegedly designed to slow down the fighting troops rather than kill en masse.

The tunnel kitchens had ingenious devices to get rid of smoke. It would pass through three or four chambers, each several yards away from the previous one, emitting a little smoke to the outside world at each chamber. The smoke was hardly detectable. I saw one in use as a demonstration, and I had to look very carefully to detect any smoke. By having several chambers disposing of the smoke, it meant that the last chamber, which emitted the most smoke was at least one hundred yards away from the kitchen and also the tunnel, should the smoke be spotted and a direct bomb attack launched. The leaves around the chamber exits would eventually become black and sooty with the smoke so they were changed each day to continue the disguise of the secret exits.

There was a room displaying model figures working on ammunitions, melting down metal to make spikes and other weapons. One display showed a couple of Vietnamese dismantling an unexploded bomb to extract the explosives for their own use. This was done by one person sawing through the bomb whilst another poured water over it to keep it cooled and prevent sparks. Sometimes however, there would be a spark and they would explode with obvious disastrous consequences. Jung told me that this was how his father had lost his eyesight during the war.

There was a large "collection" of bombs and empty shells in one corner of the room. Jung explained that this represented the average weight of bomb metal found per square metre across the Cu Chi region. It was huge. The whole place must have been at least ankle deep in metal.

One of the tunnels had the entrance widened to allow (us larger!) tourists down to experience life underground. It was awful. Very hot, humid, dank smelling. I was on my knees just to be able to crawl through the tunnel. Even taking my European size into account, it must have been extremely difficult for the Vietnamese to move along with any speed, yet they did. The tunnel I tried must have only been about a hundred feet long, and I'm not one to suffer claustrophobia, but one hundred feet was quite sufficient to have had the experience.

I was then shown air vents dotted around the woods. To the untrained eye they just looked like rocks, but when examined closely, you could see the ventilation holes. Each part of a tunnel would have had at least 2 vents. Hot air would rise out of one, thereby drawing fresh air in through the other. To deter US troops and sniffer dogs from finding the air vents, the VietCong would sprinkle pepper around the areas. They even used America soap to wash with so as to try and disguise their natural Asian body scent from the sniffer dogs.

At the end of the tour there was a video show comprising old black and white footage of the Cu Chi people leading happy, relatively prosperous farming lives before the war, and then showing them building the tunnels, and ultimately defending their territory. Clearly full strength propaganda but having now visited the tunnels, I did have a degree of admiration for the VietCong's ingenuity in their design, and also for living in them. There are always at least two sides to every story, however one of Ho Chi Minh's quotations resonated with me *"[ref the USA] if they want to make war for twenty years then we shall make war for twenty years. If they want to make peace, we shall make peace and invite them to afternoon tea."* If only that had been possible, if only Ho Chi Minh hadn't died so early when he was pushing for peace, then literally millions of lives may well have been saved.

We found a seat in a little cafe and ordered a couple of Cokes. I asked Jung to continue with the history lesson.

"Where was I up to?" he asked

"You'd told me about Agent Orange and the other chemicals deployed," I replied.

"Ah yes. Well, despite the Americans using chemical weapons such as the toxic herbicide, Agent Orange and Napalm, the communist forces fought back with anti-aircraft guns and fighter jets supplied by their Soviet and Chinese allies, and the Americans made little progress.

"On the 31st January 1968 the North Vietnamese Army and VietCong launched a large-scale offensive during the Vietnamese holiday of Tet. They had staged an assault elsewhere as a decoy, and then had the main offensive which was surprise simultaneous assaults attacking 36 provincial capitals and five of the six major cities, including Saigon where they penetrated the US embassy compound. The communist forces however failed to hold any cities for more than a few days, apart from the city of Hue which they held for three weeks and they suffered heavy losses.

"Although the fighting on the ground had been a hollow victory for the VietCong due to its lack of sustainability, it had a bigger impact across the ocean, as the offensive hit US public opinion hard, with graphic film footage of the fighting reinforcing concerns about casualties. Political support for President Johnson waned and he called for peace talks, which didn't happen. The next president, Nixon, sought an exit strategy that would leave US credibility intact and he started withdrawing troops, which left the remaining troops, continually bombarded by the VietCong, demoralised. US public hostility rose against its government especially as reports of battles gave conflicting results, or even worse, battles where ground was gained and many lives lost, only for the remaining troops to retreat soon after each small victory. The public saw just a futile loss of life after life after life. It wasn't just the American losses that turned the public against the war, but also evidence that started emerging about some of their behaviour, such as the massacre at My Lai, which you will find out more about when you visit the northern area, where US forces gang raped the women and slaughtered more than five hundred innocent unarmed Vietnamese villagers during an assault on camps they suspected to house VietCong.

"The VietCong's greatest strength was the fact that they could not be found. They walked among the ordinary people and were impossible to spot. US troops tried to counter this by clearing villages, regardless of their political affiliation, often simply burning them down, and over 1 million civilians were killed. Both the Vietnamese and American public found it hard to believe that the use of these tactics was necessary.

"Talks were happening in Paris whilst the fighting continued unabated. Eventually an agreement was reached that the US would withdraw its troops and South Vietnam would have the right to determine its own future. The last American troops left in March 1973, but a "post-war war" continued with both southern and northern forces accusing each other of breaking the agreed terms. It was awful. It just went on and on. Fighting between the north and the south continued though not as intensely as previously, and with fewer casualties.

"As American aid to South Vietnam decreased, the southern government became progressively weaker. In early March 1975,

Hanoi launched the first phase of an offensive to take the whole country. The South Vietnamese army crumbled faster than expected, and in seven weeks communist forces had swept through the south taking the central highlands and the east coast. Millions of refugees fled towards Saigon. However, Saigon was stuck in the middle as it was also in the path of the North Vietnamese Army and soon it was surrounded and being shelled constantly, regardless of whether targets were military or civilian areas. So you see, we were just as bad as the Americans, not distinguishing between troops and civilians.

"On the 29th of April the US ordered the helicopter evacuation of 7,000 American administrators and South Vietnamese from the city. Refugees battled to join the exodus, and the pictures of people crying and clawing at the embassy gates to be helped out of the country are well known and depicted in many movies. Very quickly the northern troops marched into Saigon unopposed, and the city was renamed Ho Chi Minh City, even though Ho Chi Minh had died in 1969. It is so sad that he never saw peace."

There was a silence between us as I digested all of this information and Jung reflected on it. It was probably only a minute at the most, but felt much longer.

I'd seen a very different side to the war than I'd ever come across before, and not entirely unsurprisingly, ended the tour with a very different perspective. I had learned that Vietnam had been constantly raided, occupied and partitioned throughout its history, by the Chinese, then Japanese, French and Americans.

There was a poster on the wall. A photograph of a plaque from the Museum of History which read:

"All men were created equal. They were endowed by their creator with certain inalienable rights: amongst these were life, liberty and the pursuit of happiness"

Surely nobody could disagree with that. They were words that could have been taken out of the foundation of the American Constitution, or post the French Revolution, but indeed these words were written in 1945 by Ho Chi Minh. From what I'd learned that day, I felt sure that Uncle Ho, as the Vietnamese reverently called him, was a peaceful man at heart.

We headed back to the city after a truly amazing and eye opening outing and stopped by a little farmhouse en-route where the family were making rice paper. It was all made by hand in a not dissimilar manner to making a crepe. The circular sheets of rice paper were then laid out on bamboo stretchers to dry. They exported the rice paper in addition to selling it locally for dim sum, springs rolls and the like. This was not a regular tourist stop, however Jung knew the family so decided to pop in, say hi and take me with him. There was nothing for sale there, nor did they want a donation for having shown me around. They were just extremely proud to share their little factory with me.

We also stopped at a lacquer shop where I witnessed the complex process of making lacquered wood. They were making three different types; painted, mother of pearl and eggshell. Each one went through numerous stages of being painted and sanded down and all the sanding was done by hand. The eggshell makers were especially skilled as they took tiny pieces of eggshell, chipping off minute slivers until the piece matched the gap on the picture they were making, prior to it being varnished. Here as one would expect, they had a beautiful gift shop and I was sorely tempted by a large black and white silhouette of a man fishing from a junk, but it was sixty dollars and possibly a little large and heavy for the suitcase. Yes, I was very tempted, but it was too early in the holiday to start splashing out on expensive souvenirs especially those that were somewhat awkward to carry. Furthermore, I didn't know what else I was going to see over the next couple of weeks, so needed to pace myself.

Back in the city for lunch, I couldn't believe I had seen so much in just one morning. I was deposited inside a restaurant and the guide and driver went off to eat somewhere else. The meal was a set menu. It was interesting but not especially enjoyable. The starter was a pomela spicy salad, which I expected to enjoy following my introduction to the fruit at breakfast, however served with spices it was pretty disgusting, and I left most of it. The diced prawns moulded onto bamboo sticks served with a dip were tasty, as was the sea bass served on a banana leaf, although this dish was just a tad too hot for me with the over enthusiastic addition of red chillies. Noodle soup with shrimp and vegetables, cooked and served at my table was the best course. I declined the crème caramel as I had never been overly keen on squidgy desserts.

Jung was somewhat amused by the number of cameras I had with me and I explained the rationale. Today I had used the camcorder for the first time and realised that I should have practiced a little before coming away. I knew that when I played it back there were going to be some lovely dark shots where I'd forgotten to take the lens cap off, or moving ground pictures where I had slung it over my shoulder and forgotten to turn it off. Thank goodness for editing software.

Jung asked me what I did for a living and I told him that I worked for ICI paints in marketing. The company had only been in Vietnam for a couple of years, but he said that he always uses ICI paints (didn't they all say that I thought), but then he went on to say that our "Gecko" ad was one of his favourites and described it in amazing detail. In turn he explained this to the driver, whose English was very limited, and the driver became very animated as well, wriggling his hands in the air to demonstrate the geckoes sliding down the wall. Wow, what impact and recall. ICI Vietnam should be well pleased.

English was not widely spoken at all, and I had some difficulty making myself understood to anyone other than Jung. Jung constantly translated for the driver so that he was not excluded from our conversations. At lunch for example, the waitress tried very hard, but kept calling me Sir.

With lunch completed, the history tour of the holiday continued with a visit to the Reunification Palace, the former Presidential Palace (Dinh Thong Nhet). It was now a museum with deep historical relevance, as this was where on the 30th of April 1975, the communist tanks burst through the gates and overthrew the South

Vietnamese government. It was a peaceful coup with the government surrendering without argument.

Inside was only moderately interesting. The ex-state banqueting hall, combat strategy rooms, foreign guests reception rooms and so on had little appeal. However, standing on the rooftop and looking down at the gates, I could just imagine the tanks bursting through nearly 30 years earlier.

I asked Jung if the old US embassy was still standing, where there was the famous footage of the last helicopter leaving from the roof and hundreds of southern Vietnamese wanting to escape, but being left behind. The answer was no. Apparently, when Madeleine Albright visited she was so horrified to see how many tourists gathered to gawp at the building, which was of huge historical embarrassment to the American government, that she ordered it to be bulldozed and a Consulate erected in its place.

We then paid a visit to old Saigon, the first stop being the central post office. It was a beautiful old French colonial building with high vaulted ceilings, cavernous and spacious with ornate pillars. I was amused to see in the centre, a table with bowls of paste and brushes. The locals used these to stick down their envelopes as self-sealing envelopes were too expensive for most. I watched one local doing it and it took me back to infant school and Blue Peter sticky-backed plastic projects.

I meandered over to a book shop nearby to get some colourful postcards, then to a street vendor where I bought what initially looked like a pristine copy of The Quiet American. However, on flipping through the pages I rapidly realised that it was a photocopy. What the hell, it only cost me a couple of quid, and what an appropriate book to read whilst in Saigon.

The final stop of the day was at The War Remnants museum. Outside there were numerous tanks, helicopters, bits of bombs and aircraft parts, none of which especially interested me. Inside there were six small exhibition halls showing photographs depicting different aspects of the American war. It was well kept and well presented, and told a convincing story of a country devastated by modern war.

Jung warned me before I went in that I may find some of the photos disturbing, and that he would wait outside to allow me to walk around the exhibition halls at my own pace. To say that some of the photos "may be disturbing" was a gross understatement. They showed the harsh reality of war and a reminder of what humans are capable of inflicting on each other. One of the halls had photos of American soldiers torturing and mutilating women, children and old people included. One of the most distressing was a picture of 4 American soldiers squatting by the decapitated bodies of their victims, holding their severed heads in the air. One of the soldiers was grinning. Another photo showed a soldier holding up the remains of a victim's body after a bombing attack. There was a head attached to a small portion of torso and one arm. It was truly gruesome. It was very noticeable how quiet the visitors became as they walked through the exhibition rooms.

Another exhibition hall showed the effects of Agent Orange and other defoliating chemicals on both the landscape and the population. People and unborn babies were revoltingly disfigured by their effects. The same room showed the effects of Napalm and some of the poor sods photographed would have been better to have died as their range of injuries were exceptionally sickening and life changing.

The last exhibition room showed the modern day, and people horrifically maimed from unexploded landmines. The poor farmer tilling his land; the little girl playing by the river. On average there was one person killed each day by bombs still remaining. 400 had died the previous year in 2002 and ironically, many of the mines were left by the VietCong.

A few tears oozed from my eyes and dribbled down my cheeks as I took in the range of pictures. They were as distressing as those in the Yad Veshem holocaust memorial museum outside Jerusalem, yet there was a morbid curiosity that drew you to them. I think it's that the brain can't immediately take in the horror, so you have to keep looking until your brain registers that they were indeed real photographs showing real atrocities.

Back at the hotel, I did cry when reflecting on the excursion to the museum, confronting you so visually with some of humanity's darker moments. I had only been in Vietnam a little over a day and had already taken to this country and its people even though it had been especially exhausting and harrowing at times. I was glad to have seen another side to Vietnam, and especially the American war. I won't be able to watch the Deer Hunter again without thinking about the "other side" of the tale.

I dropped off my day-bag and headed out to buy an overnight bag. The next day I would be staying overnight in the Mekong Delta but would be returning to Saigon the day after, so it made sense to store my main suitcase at the hotel and just take a smaller bag with sufficient stuff for an overnight stay.

I had another great adventure crossing the roads of Saigon. Luckily the traffic didn't move too fast. It was a case of taking a deep breath, stepping out, and hoping that none of the 14 streams of motorbikes or mopeds hit you. I had a few false starts where I stepped out and then quickly retreated. A bike went past me with both the rider and passenger window-shopping whilst riding forwards. I crossed about 4 main roads and exchanged grins with locals standing and watching this foreigner navigating with difficulty what they did with ease. One young lady clapped and smiled when I succeeded with one of my crossings.

I decided that whilst I was out, I'd find a restaurant to eat in to make a change from the hotel. I found one. A woman was sitting outside at the door. She couldn't speak any English, so I gesticulated that I was going inside to eat, grinning at her. She grinned back. The room was like a ballroom full of round tables with families sitting around jabbering to each other. I wandered around to see if that solo table was waiting for me somewhere. No, it was fully packed. I wandered out and smiled again to the lady at the door, shaking my head. Next was a hotel and after that another restaurant. I had a similar non-verbal conversation with that lady sitting at the door before I wandered in, but again, no spare tables.

I backtracked to the hotel I'd just passed. They must surely have somewhere to eat. The receptionist spoke a little English, and I asked if they had a restaurant. She said they had two, and pointed to the two outside that I'd just been in, but she went on to say that sorry, tonight they were being used for wedding parties, so were not open as restaurants. Yes, I had just gate crashed two weddings in less than five minutes. No wonder the ladies at the door were smiling at me. Or were they laughing?

I felt amazingly good out on the streets of Saigon. There was no pestering, everyone smiled at me and I smiled back. People said hello, and I said hello back. I felt safer than I did back home on the streets of Aylesbury, and by now it was dark, with poor street lighting. But it wasn't just feeling good out on the streets, I felt great within myself. Not one pang of loneliness, and lots of affection for myself. I felt confident and contented, something I rarely felt back home. I think this holiday was already proving to be very good for my health and mental well-being. Definitely a good day. No, a great day. Wow if that was day one, what did the rest of the holiday have in store.

I checked my e-mail back at the hotel. I had a response from the British Embassy. Unfortunately they didn't have a Rupert registered as an Expat, although they went on to say that didn't necessarily mean he wasn't living there. There were also Christmas wishes from a variety of people who claimed to be sending no cards that year but would be making a donation to charity instead. I wondered how many actually would.

There was an email from Stephen, still waiting to hear from Alan and Jack reference their availability for my dad's birthday party the following year. Stephen was a friend who also had a jazz trio and I wanted them to play at my dad's seventieth, the party being my gift to him. As his birthday was only a few weeks away, I had to carry on organising it from a distance. In his email, Stephen admitted to having eaten dog, knowingly. (UGH!!), but he had never tried snake. It crossed my mind that I would have to get him one of the ghastly bottles of snake wine that I'd seen in the shops. The liquor (allegedly) cures all ailments and each bottle contained at least one dead snake.

There was also an amusing mail from Bob. I hadn't heard from him for a couple of years. We were at university together and it said:

"Merry Christmas. Bet you find it hard to believe you're forty-seven. I've just turned forty-eight. Don't know where time goes. Still married, still working in Northamptonshire. Love Bob. P.S. Do you still have the best breasts at Warwick?"

I replied,

"Cheeky bugger! I'm only forty-five. Currently in Vietnam on holiday. Merry Christmas, Love Susan. P.s. Ref my breasts; I couldn't possibly comment!"

Mekong Delta - 22nd December

The light was flashing on my room phone. There was a message for me. I called the reception and they asked me to call at the front desk because they had a problem with the traveller's cheques that I had cashed the day before.

My legs were aching a little from all the walking yesterday, especially after crawling through the tunnel.

I stopped off at reception en-route to breakfast. They thought that their bank wouldn't accept my cheques so they needed to have their money back. I told them to phone the travellers cheque 24 hours hotline as I was going to have my breakfast.

Over breakfast I wondered what would happen if I refused to give them the cash back? However, when I dropped off my suitcase for overnight storage, nothing more was said about the cheques, so I worked on the assumption that "no news was good news".

To be fair, the cheques were actually quite confusing. They were called Euro Travellers Cheques, but they were in sterling. They were also stamped Thomas Cook. I could see why confusion with the branding could occur. I decided that it might be worth changing more money at the next hotel just in case I got caught short or found myself with a similar dilemma. I was still somewhat mystified at the issue with my cheques as I was staying in supposedly the best hotel in Vietnam, and I couldn't possibly be the first person to use such cheques there.

I was waiting outside for my pick up and Jung was impressed with my promptness, as usually he had to phone the rooms to wake people up, and then hang around whilst they got their acts together. It was around 70 degrees and only a little humid, pretty much perfect sightseeing weather. I was unlikely to come back with a deep tan, even though I had been wearing shorts and T-shirts since arriving. Today's itinerary was a journey down to the Mekong Delta for a boat trip and overnight stay at Can Tho.

I gleaned more information from Jung during the journey though some things may have changed now as this was back in 2003.

I saw a small group of young girls chattering animatedly as they made their way to school. The were wearing pristine blue pinafore dresses with crisp white cotton shirts, their glossy black hair perfectly plaited into two pigtails with the parting as straight as if it had been cut with a knife. Some had leather school bags on their backs, and others were carrying their books under their arms. Only a mile further on we passed a small shack house with rickety wooden supports and a corrugated tin roof. Four children of school age were playing with stones and sticks by the roadside.

"Jung" I questioned, "How come that some of the children seem to be going to school whilst others are playing by the roadside?"

"Education is complicated here." He paused a moment before continuing,

"Theoretically it is compulsory, but you have to pay for it. The poor people however clearly can't afford it."

46

"So what is the penalty if they don't go to school, I mean, if it's compulsory then surely they have to find a way or be punished?"

"Don't worry, they are not thrown into jail, but a blind eye is turned instead. In the cities and towns the wealthy kids go to school from 7.30am to 4.00pm. In the countryside there are three shifts because there are not enough schools or enough teachers. The government's target is to get it down to two shifts per day, but there are already fifty to sixty kids per class. The children you have just seen playing are probably on an afternoon or early shift for schooling."

Health care, as with education, had to be paid for. If you were taken ill or were in an accident, the hospital would contact your relatives for a deposit before they would commence treatment. And this was a communist country?

Jung told me that one of his friends was dying of a blood clot on the brain. He went on to explain that his friend had never smoked, didn't drink, did plenty of exercise, ate healthily etc and was only in his mid thirties. Jung then said that he himself smoked, drank (he claimed to drink fifteen to twenty cans of beer or a litre of whisky in one session, however as he neither looked nor smelt like a heavy drinker, I suspected there was a large dose of embellishment there), didn't exercise, ate the wrong foods, and had women, but was totally fit and healthy. I commented on his "had women" as I thought he was married? Yes, he was married and had two kids, but had the occasional woman on the side. He suspected that I was a little disapproving of this revelation, so hastily explained that he lived up to very high standards. He never had, nor would, touch drugs and he wouldn't have sex with a virgin. Some morals.

The average salary just didn't exist. The average household outgoing on electricity, fuel, food and essentials was around one hundred pounds a month. The government minimum salary was twenty pounds a month. I questioned whether that meant that the majority of people in Vietnam were in horrendous debt?

"Not really," Jung explained, "as they have concessions for certain groups of people for their cost of living, so this boosts the average salary."

However, the sums still didn't make sense. Jung said that he believed the average salary per month was actually around three hundred pounds, but it was very difficult to say as it was a cash economy. Most people had several jobs. It was only government jobs and big corporations where salary records were kept, hence the difficulty to tax people and to know with any degree of accuracy how much people were earning. It was common for people working for the government or large companies to have low wages, so they would turn up for work, use the company phones to make all their personal phone calls and then nip out or become invisible for an hour or so, when they would be doing another business transaction elsewhere to boost their salary. I wondered if this happened at ICI Vietnam? Jung had several jobs, but he said that it was not surprising in his line of work because tourism was seasonal. He was a freelance tour guide for Destination Asia, an English teacher and a translator for businesses.

The journey down to the Mekong Delta was a little slow and the scenery, although pretty and interesting for the first ten miles, became somewhat repetitive being mainly paddy fields broken by the occasional clump of trees.

During the journey I told Jung about my "crossing the road experience" the night before, and apparently I had the correct approach, just step out and slowly cross, and nobody would hit you. However, you should never ever stop, hesitate or step backwards under any circumstances as the motor vehicles were so used to avoiding pedestrians by judging their forward propelling speed, that if you deviated from this modus operandi it confused the drivers and then you were almost certainly going to cause an accident, probably involving yourself. I tried it out later in the day, and it worked.

We stopped en-route at what I guessed was their equivalent of a service station. There were little thatched huts selling cola and souvenirs with a few cages of monkeys and snakes dotted around for tourists to ogle at. I had been photographing signs which read funny to an English speaker, and there was a sign on one of the monkey cages that in Vietnamese said "Please keep out of the monkeys' cage", but the English translation underneath was actually "please keep out of the monkeys' case".

We arrived at the quayside at My Tho to board the boat for my first Mekong Delta trip. There was a queue of tourists waiting to get on the boats which were simple covered affairs with seating for around thirty. I found myself hoping to get a good seat, that typical "tourist panic" akin to wanting the one dryer in a laundrette when you spend the last ten minutes looking at everyone's washing machines hoping that yours will complete first. I looked around at the people in the queue and thought that they didn't especially look like the sort of people I'd have wanted to have been in a group with, so I was not only perfectly contented to be by myself but at this moment I was actually glad to be by myself.

There were several tourist groups and within each were most definitely clones. The Italian group comprised more women than men and were generally elderly ladies dressed in finery suitable for a formal lunch, not a boat trip. They were heavily made up most having dark slashes above their eyes where their eyebrows had once lived. Most were smoking and all were very loud. Nobody was listening because they were all talking. The English group, that I'd most likely have been joined with if I'd booked correctly comprised of 16 people. There was the young timid honeymoon couple I'd seen at breakfast the day before, standing a little apart from the others clinging to each other like limpets, only releasing their grip to smear more sun cream on their arms. They didn't talk to each other. They didn't need to as their gooey eyes said it all. There were three girls travelling together, all with pale complexions and wide brimmed sun hats, not a trace of make-up. They huddled together not speaking as they each studied their individual guide books. They looked as if this was their first venture out of their homes back in England, but they were probably quiet, studious, dull university students. The rest of the group were middle aged couples. They were all dressed in what I'd call "smart casual", definitely taking more care over their appearance than I did. The men were mainly wearing sand coloured trousers and some had sleeveless safari jackets to match, the type with numerous pockets to store stuff, but then you could never remember what you'd stored in which pocket, so a lot of fiddling about was going on as they searched for their boat tickets. The women were generally coiffured, wore short sleeved cotton shirts and either floral Laura Ashley skirts or pale coloured slacks. A couple were wearing brand new trainers, clearly bought for the holiday and yet to attract any dust. The other women were wearing inappropriate. designer style summer sandals and several of the men were wearing walking sandals together with white ankle socks. I was in my walking boots. They looked bored, and that made them look boring. There wasn't a spark of adventure amongst them and one was loudly complaining about how early they had to rise and that no English food had been offered at dinner the night before.

Yes, I was extremely glad to be travelling alone and not as part of their group.

As I was inwardly saying thank you, thank you, thank you for not putting me with this group, Jung interrupted my thoughts and asked me to stand aside and let the other people on the boats first. There were five boats moored next to each other. To reach the second you had to climb over the first and so on. My heart sank. I was going to be the last person on the boat which would mean that I'd get the crummy seat with no view and an overdose of diesel fumes. Then my heart lifted again as we clambered over the four boats, to the fifth, and there was nobody else in it, the whole boat was just for me. I exclaimed that I was surprised and Jung told me that on this holiday everything was "just for me," except the hotels.

Having witnessed my potential travel companions, I was suddenly so very glad not to be a part of a tour and I was sure that the opportunities I was having to chat with Jung and also some of the places he'd taken me to already, off the beaten track, such as the rice paper farm, I wouldn't had benefited from had I been in a group. This holiday was turning out to be wonderful.

The boat trip was fantastic, going from the main river and then down the smaller tributaries, some of them no wider than a British road. I hardly knew what to film next. Glimpses of the agricultural life on the banks, fishermen and women with a simple net trying to catch whatever they could, huts on stilts with palm leaf roofs, the beautiful greenery of the surrounding countryside, the paddy fields, the banana groves, the palm trees, bamboo "factories", children playing by the water's edge. It was a photographer's paradise.

I was visiting the Mekong at the right time as for most of the year it was either flooded or in drought, and I was told that during the flood season, an average of one child per hour was killed. This was another statistic that I took with a pinch of salt, assuming it to be a Jung exaggeration, however research when I returned home showed that drowning is the major cause of death of children in Vietnam, and his estimates were not far out.

We stopped off at a little village where the locals were making sweets. Toffee sweets, sticky rice cakes, popped rice and other candies. They popped the rice in a wok of gargantuan proportions, with sand in the bottom. They used un-milled rice and so the sand was used as an abrasive to break down the outer shell. The sand had been burned black from being used so many times. A man

52

stirred the cauldron of rice and sand vigorously until all the rice had popped. He then sifted out the sand into another large wok, ready to be used again. I was amazed that the popped rice once sifted had no sand in it at all. I bought some packets of the sweets and toffees to take back as gifts for the office staff and friends.

One thing I liked about the trip so far, well, there were lots I liked about the trip so far, but I was seeing different local handicrafts compared to other places I'd visited in the world. I'd seen enough spice and rubber plantations as well as batik works and people making coir mats and carvings to last a lifetime, so it was refreshing to see alternative crafts.

We meandered down the river for a couple of hours before stopping at a lovely picturesque restaurant for lunch set amongst the trees. I was shown to my table, which was set apart from the rest of the restaurant, in a modest raised area, one table, one chair, set for one. It was magical. It looked like the equivalent of a honeymoon setting. However, instead of feeling that there should be someone with me to share this exceptional moment, I just felt honoured to have been given what was obviously the best table in the restaurant. Jung and the driver didn't eat with me. They went off to the back of the restaurant, where they would be given something to eat for free for bringing in a paying customer, so I guess I was indirectly buying them lunch. This was the most perfect setting I had ever had lunch in, and the lunch was exquisite, both in display and taste. A most excellent meal. Succulent grilled sea bass, giant prawns seared to perfection in garlic and spices, little spring rolls erupting with flavour, aromatic soup, perfumed rice and the most tender soy sauce marinated pork loin. Had I died and gone to heaven?

In the afternoon we drove down to the southern Mekong tributary, crossed over on a ferry and headed to the Victoria Hotel at Can Tho. This was a stunning hotel set in its own grounds by the river. It was relatively new but had been built in a colonial style with lots of wood everywhere and it was extremely comfortable. Jung left me at 4.00pm to my own devices for the rest of the afternoon and evening and said that he would collect me very early in the morning.

The town of Can Tho was a courtesy boat ride away, so I had time to go and explore. Yet again, I found the people very friendly, welcoming and smiley, and then I suddenly realised that I was walking around with a permanent smile on my face, and it had spread up to my eyes and radiated my delight of just being here. I was feeling incredibly uplifted.

I had an interesting walk around the small town, through the fresh produce markets and down past the local shops.

A large statue of Ho Chi Minh was smiling and waving proudly in the main square.

I bought some incense sticks and headed back to the quayside for the courtesy boat back to the hotel, but it was nowhere in sight. I saw an outside cafe not far away so went over to have a drink whilst waiting for the boat. It was like a doll's house, full of miniature tables and chairs. The sort of kiddie plastic chairs you can buy in B&Q. They were for Vietnamese sized people and I only just managed to fit into one of them. I then had THE most disgusting coffee I'd ever had. Unfortunately the staff didn't speak any English. I tried to order a coffee with milk, no sugar. What arrived was a cup of jet black, thick glupey coffee with at least a tablespoon of condensed milk in it. I tipped it out into the grass when nobody was looking.

Time to go back to the quayside and wait for the boat. As the boat didn't appear I turned my mobile phone on to call the hotel to ask them to send the boat. I had some text messages from Joe, which had been fairly recently sent, so I gave him a quick call to let him know that I was having the most perfect holiday. He was not in good form; woman troubles, and he had been drinking even though it must only have been about 10.00am UK time, and as I was so ebullient I really didn't want a drunken conversation now. Luckily, the boat then arrived to take me back to the hotel, so I told Joe that I would catch up with him later.

By 6.30pm, I had showered and changed into my pale pink Indian outfit to go down to dinner, it was the only smart outfit I had taken with me and it was cool and wispy to wear as well as being light for the suitcase kilos. It was a Salwar kameez, a flowing top and long baggy pants in a very fine soft cotton. In England it would look like I'd gone out in my pyjamas, but in Asia it was de rigueur.

En-route to the restaurant I picked up my e-mails. Great, it looked like I had a date for my dad's party, so I phoned the manager at the Historic Quays whom I'd had a good old banter with before the holiday and he was highly amused to take his first booking from Vietnam, although he said that he'd been to the Mekong Delta, and knew exactly where I was as he had stayed in the very same hotel. It was only about six weeks away and I had to coordinate the venue with Stephen's trio availability and of course my father's availability. I couldn't leave it until I got home as I might have lost the provisional booking, hence dealing with it via emails and a few phones calls whilst on holiday. I know there will be some people who baulk at the thought of me checking my emails each day whilst on holiday, however it's great when you are travelling alone to know that in reality you are no further away than twelve inches of phone wire from your friends.

For dinner I opted for the outside tables in the restaurant. Others came out, but after being bitten by mozzies, as the hotel was right next to the riverbank, they retreated rapidly inside. I stuck it out for the duration. They were not that bad and I had liberally sprayed my ankles and arms with mosquito repellent, (famous last words I thought. Bet I'd look like I'd suffered terminal chicken pox the next day and scratching like I was lice ridden).

The meal was up to the standard I'd now gotten used to in Vietnam and the only thing that marred the evening was a god-awful pianist in the lounge, who I could unfortunately hear from where I was sitting. He was "trying" to play some classics using a version akin to the Lilac series (simplified classics), plus some well know popular numbers. However, he played everything slowly and deliberately as if he was sight reading the music for the first time, sounding like he was fumbling to find the next note, and when he made a mistake he went back and played the bar again rather than carrying on and letting the moment pass. Shame that I had left my keyboard in the suitcase in Saigon, not that I'd had an opportunity to use it yet. You will now be wondering why I had a keyboard in my suitcase. Well, as I was starting to learn jazz and improvisation, I'd bought a small two octave kids lightweight plastic keyboard to practice on whenever I had a little spare time and wherever I found myself, and somehow it had found its way into my suitcase when I was packing.

After a dessert of delicious mixed fresh fruits, I retired to my room. I needed to be up early the next day to catch the tide for the floating market. Jung was coming with a boat to collect me at 6.00am, so there would be no time for breakfast.

The Floating Market - 23rd December

For Pete's sake, I was awake early yet again at 4.00am waiting for the alarm to go off at 5.15. This wasn't just jet leg but also that personal alarm clock embedded deep in your subconscious that is all too aware of when you need an early start and never quite let's you drift into deep sleep just in case some other brain function decides to overrule it. I didn't go back to sleep. No insect bites from the previous evening, but my legs were still aching a little from the tunnels, and I also discovered a huge bruise on my knee, probably also from the tunnels, but none of this dampened my spirits in the slightest and I headed straight down to the hotel jetty to wait for Jung and the boat.

At spot on 6.00am they arrived, though what a hoot reaching the boat. I had to walk down a gang plank precariously hanging in mid air by a fraying rope; then step into a very small unstable boat; then clamber over some floating oil drums tentatively strapped together, and then finally scramble into my boat. It took some doing with my day bag on my back and my camera case slung around my neck, but surprisingly I made it in one piece and bone dry.

Usually the tourists were taken straight to the floating market and then back to their hotels again. Jung, however, had his own circular route that went up through the narrow tributaries to see the countryside awakening, then round and home via the floating market. It sounded good to me, and he knew his territory.

I guessed the river was pretty polluted considering what I saw some of the locals doing in it, but despite this, it was an extremely picturesque journey with lots of greenery, trees and small thatched farms. Periodically there were narrow crossings over the river called "monkey bridges". They were exceedingly thin bridges made from bamboo and some were only two bamboo poles in width, yet the locals navigated them on foot, with cycles and pushing carts as if it were a dual carriageway with excess space.

After going down the tributary for some way, Jung asked if I want to get out and have a walk. The boat owner's daughter, whose name I couldn't pronounce but meant Velvet in English, came along too. She was 13 and a little chatterbox, but spoke no English, yet the two of us set up an amazingly comprehensive sign language conversation. She no longer went to school because her parents couldn't afford to send her, so she sold souvenirs to tourists. We walked over one of the wider monkey bridges, about two feet wide with no railings to hold on to. Bikers, cyclists and pedestrians from the villages were using it en-route to work without any difficulty at all, passing each other in opposite directions without even hesitating. I felt certain that I was going to end up in the river, but for the second time that day stayed amazingly dry.

We walked away from the river into the forest and came across a small marigold farm. The owners were perfectly happy to let me wander around their little plantation. I asked Jung what the Vietnamese was for "thank you." It's "Cam on," however he added that I was better off sticking to English. He explained that many words in Vietnamese were spelt the same but depending on

60

intonation had totally different meanings. He pronounces some of them for me and the difference to my ear was barely perceptible. "Cam on," with a very very slightly different intonation means "SHUT UP!!!!!". Not wanting to offend, I decided to stick with English and use hand gestures and facial expressions to convey my thanks. They refused a tip for showing me around. Their pleasure came from showing off the fruits of their labour. Then back to the boat and on to the floating market.

Wow – stunning – spectacular – dramatic – another world, I ran out of adjectives to describe the floating market experience. There were literally hundreds of boats selling their wares, mainly fresh produce, although there were also little old women in smaller boats weaving in and out of the bigger boats, selling tea and breakfast rolls. It was just like any bustling market but on the water. The boats had spires with their produce spiked on the top like giant vertical kebabs, so that buyers could easily make their way to the appropriate boat for their purchases. Another Kodak moment, indeed a hundred Kodak moments. There were a few bumps and knocks as our boat wended its way through the busy thoroughfare. It stalled on a couple of occasions and the owner pulled the propeller pole out of the water, removed some debris - usually a plastic bag that had become tangled up - then started it up again.

There were other larger boats with groups of tourists, and not for the first time I thought, although it was an accident that I ended up being by myself, I was again so glad that I wasn't in a group. I made a mental note that this was the way to travel in the future.

The most amusing of the tourist group boats was one with Japanese people in it. They were all wearing bright orange life jackets, the only group to be doing so. It looked so incongruent, like mini Belisha beacons propped up in a boat.

I had no doubt that none of my photos, not even the camcorder, would do justice to the ambience and atmosphere of this trip through the floating market. I was only just getting used to the fade in and out on the camcorder after reading the manual at dinner last night. Typical me, play around with something new, try and figure out how it works, then when all else fails, read the instructions. I believed that I now had it sussed.

We approached a huge boat selling sugar beet. They invited me to climb on board where I had a superb panoramic view of the floating market. Brill!! They also gave me some sugar beet to try which I found more palatable than sugar cane which I had tried previously. I tried to tip them but they refused. Jung told me that it was their pleasure to invite me on to their boat and let me sample their wares.

The floating market visit was over, but Jung asked the boatman to go back through once more for me, where I sat and soaked up the ambience rather than take more pictures, and then we headed back to the hotel.

I was starting to develop a very sore throat and it felt like I'd been gargling rusty razor blades. I think it was a combination of the traffic fumes in Saigon and the boat fumes in the market. I didn't feel like I was going down with anything specific, but at some point I needed to top up my throat lozenge supply as it was starting to run a little low.

Back at the hotel for 8.30am, breakfast, then the drive back to Saigon. As the boat approached the hotel, Velvet tried to sell me a Vietnamese silk top. Unfortunately they didn't have my size in the colour I wanted, blue. Jung said that was no problem as whilst I was having breakfast they would go back to the town and fetch one for me, so I padded off to the dining room.

Following a substantial breakfast, I collected my overnight bag and was ready to head back to Saigon. We were just about to leave the hotel when I said to Jung

"Oh, did they manage to get me a shirt in the right size?"

"Oh no!" he exclaimed, "They are probably still waiting for you by the jetty. Sorry, I forgot to go back and see if they could find something."

I left him by the car and hot footed it down to the jetty. Velvet wasn't there, but her mother was. We used sign language to communicate that, no she didn't have a shirt, what size was I, five in Vietnamese sizing, she'd go and get one. I indicated five minutes with my fingers tapping on my watch, and the boat disappeared. After five minutes, Jung came looking for me as he was keen to get on the road. I explained what had happened and he said we couldn't wait. I felt bad and didn't want to leave the woman in the lurch but he said that she would understand if I'd disappeared. He looked out to the river, grinned and said,

"Is that them coming back?"

"No" I replied "they were in the bigger boat." But his eyesight was better than mine as it was indeed the lady returning, but in a smaller faster boat. They had brought me a bright blue shirt, actually a size too big, but as it was only 150,000 Dong (around six pounds) I wasn't going to argue. I discovered later when opening the package at the next hotel to look at the top, that a pair of silk trousers in the same colour was included, so not a bad deal at all.

We set off back to Saigon, with a three to four hour journey ahead. Jung was doing his English homework in the back of the car. I was seated in the front for the best view and he asked me to help with some of the translations. Most Brits would have had difficulty with some of the words and phrases he was asked to translate, let alone someone learning them in a second language. Procambium, procumbent and promulgating. I reckoned that he was more than half way through the dictionary. If he passed these exams he would most certainly be a more accomplished English speaker, than most English people.

He also continued to tell me a little more about life in Vietnam. He explained that the traffic police were extremely corrupt. They could effectively stop anyone, at any time they liked, for no reason whatsoever and ask for money. They were disliked intensely by the locals and they were amongst the more wealthy Vietnamese people because of the bribes they took as a matter of course, and hence ate well and so were a tad on the portly side. They also wore mustard yellow uniforms, which is why with the colour and their

64

porcine appearance they were known colloquially as the "yellow pigs".

Vietnam had conscription at the age of eighteen for three years. However there were ways you could avoid signing up. If you were studying or had elderly parents requiring you to look after them, you could defer, but you should theoretically have completed conscription by the age of 29. Many people managed to find ways around it, or accumulate deferences, so as to avoid it altogether. Nobody however came looking for you. A common way out of conscription if you had no feasible reason to defer was to join the police force, but it was supposed to be as a career, not just for 3 years.

Jung joined the police and did 2 years training followed by one year's active service, then resigned. He explained that he was not a coward. He would fight to his last breath for his country, but at the time of his conscription the Vietnamese were fighting in Cambodia, so as it wasn't a case of defending his own country but interfering in another, and as it was a particularly nasty war and he was reluctant to die for a cause that he didn't believe in, he joined the police instead of opting for conscription.

We arrived back in Saigon around lunchtime and with the early morning start I felt as if I'd done a full day already. Lunch was at a noodle soup or Pho restaurant. There were formica tables and plastic chairs and mess everywhere, but I had delicious chicken noodle soup with the locals. Jung and the driver ate with me today. It was said to be the best noodle restaurant in Saigon, and judging by the crowds of locals waiting for a seat, I could well believe it. I love noodles and noodle soup but they are not the easiest things to consume without creating some mess, so I was a little embarrassed to see that Jung and the driver had spotlessly clean place mats at the end of the meal whereas mine, along with my shirt, showed signs of noodles that had swung unceremoniously towards my mouth.

I was dropped off at the hotel at around 2.00pm, and having checked in again only twenty four hours after I'd left, I wondered what to do with the rest of the afternoon. My throat was starting to kill me and I was now out of lozenges.

I travel with a pretty comprehensive medical kit. It had been added to and honed down over the years. For example, I stopped stocking it with Arret and Imodium ten years back when I realised that I never suffer the sort of afflictions requiring such medication. I even carry a couple of syringes and needles, left over from an old business travel medical pack, just in case I'm somewhere where needle hygiene is a little iffy. It was like an insurance policy, if I take something for every eventuality, I won't be ill. It therefore must be because I didn't pack enough sore throat tablets that I was now suffering.

I decided to have a walking trip back to the main post office to get some post card stamps which was about a mile from the hotel, and I felt sure that I would pass at least one pharmacy en-route. By now I was a dab hand at crossing the wide Saigon streets, treating the experience as if it was a round of "jeux sans frontier". I had developed a style whereby instead of looking at the on-coming traffic, which created the temptation to stop or step backwards, I

66

now looked in the opposite direction. However, I encountered a new obstacle on the sojourn - bikers riding on the pavements. There was one and only one way to avoid them. Step out of the way pretty damned quick! I reached the post office in one piece and without encountering a pharmacy. However, as I came out, my eye caught an "SOS 24 Hour Medical Centre for Foreigners" sign. I wandered in. It was a little like a mini hospital and I asked if I could just get some sore throats tablets from their pharmacy counter, something antiseptic and anti-bacterial. No problem, but the pharmacist wanted to know if I'd like to see a doctor. No, just throat lozenges please.

Two types later and about ten pounds out of pocket, I headed towards the one tourist attraction, or rather major historical site in Saigon that I hadn't visited. It was where the US Embassy used to stand and where the "famous" last helicopter left with the ambassador. On my way there I passed at least 3 pharmacies and topped up in each, so that by the time I reached the site of the old embassy I had about twenty pounds worth of cough mixture and numerous types of throat tablets. This would definitely guarantee a quick recovery.

It was quite a walk to the old site, probably another mile or so on from the post office, and Jung was absolutely correct, there was nothing to see at all except a relatively new consulate building of anonymous concrete with an American flag outside. No plaque. No reference. Nothing. On the map of Saigon I was carrying with me it was marked as "Apocalypse Now".

There were some other interesting and somewhat amusing references on the city map. It was a pretty good map, with loads of

67

information crammed onto it. Places of interest, key hotels, restaurants, etc. Most of the symbols were self explanatory, but I had to look up "INT" in the symbol section. Perhaps it was some sort of international centre or tourist information, but no, it was the Internet Cafes. The times they were a changing....

Then back to the hotel for a couple of Tiger Beers and to write the postcards. I checked my e-mails and there were further greetings from Australian relatives and a load of jokes from James. I sent him an e-mail wishing him Happy Christmas and asked him not to send me any more until the New Year when I'm back home, as he was clogging up my inbox. I deleted most of them anyway without even reading them as a continual flow of e-mail jokes had long since lost its appeal. I also confirmed the date for my dad's party to all appropriate parties. Job done.

I went down to the buffet dinner. Although I had only eaten there twice and had a night away, the young waitress breezed up to me

"Good evening madam. Usual table?"

"Yes please."

"And would madam like a Tiger beer?" I just love it when people make an effort with their level of service To make you feel special. I'd no doubt leave her a large tip.

I went to bed around 9.30pm after packing everything up, as not entirely surprisingly, the next day would be a 4.00am wake up, with a 4.45am pick up for a 6.00am flight. Wow, this holiday had some early starts and tested your mettle.

Danang and Hoi An – Christmas Eve

I didn't sleep at all well, partly because I was conscious that I had to be up at such an early hour yet again, plus I was coughing all night and my throat was worse. I grabbed a coffee and Mars Bar for "breakfast" then it was off to the airport. Jung arrived at 4.45am and I jokingly told him that this wasn't a holiday but an endurance test. However I don't think he understood the joke as I was amazed at how many people were already up and about at that time of the morning, although we did also pass people sleeping in hammocks strung like spiders webs between lampposts.

It was a relatively straightforward check in procedure and somewhat more civilized than I'd found in places like India for example, but I was quite sad to say farewell to Jung as he'd been a bloody good guide and had crammed an awful lot into my few days in the south.

You were not allowed to photograph at airports, otherwise I would have taken one of the smoking room for my "funny signs" collection as one of the smoking room signs was "Phong Hut".

It was great being on a small internal flight with the locals as they were so tiny and thin they didn't encroach on my personal space, although for them it must have been a nightmare being placed next to a European. As the lady next to me chatted to the gentleman at the other side of the aisle, I imagined her saying,

"What incredible bad luck. Only one fat English lady on the flight and I have to be seated next to her!"

The flight was about an hour long and I was served a truly disgusting sandwich that I couldn't eat. I wouldn't even know where to start to describe the filling as it definitely didn't look or smell like anything I had ever come across before.

It was an easy passage out of Danang airport, and there was a chap with a sign ready to meet me. He was the driver and he then introduced me to the guide, Jin. He was shorter and thinner than Jung, and dressed more casually having discarded the corporate tie. His hair was showing flecks of grey and his teeth were a little crooked and yellowed. He asked if I want to go for a cup of coffee or tea, I said "yes please," very eagerly, as I had missed breakfast and was a little parched after the flight, so we stopped at a local tea / coffee shop where I was served an even more disgusting coffee than the one in Can Tho.

The first coffee was brought cold, with ice in it and very black. I'd asked for a white coffee with no sugar. It was too early in the morning to be polite and just drink it so I shook my head at Jin, and explained that I'd like a hot coffee. He in turn explained to the waitress, and she returned with the exact same cup standing in a bowl of hot water. I sipped the coffee, UGH!!! It was very cold, very thick, very strong, even stronger than anything I'd ever drank in Tunisia or Turkey, and disgustingly sweet. I just couldn't drink it, so that one was sent back also. The third one arrived, still black, but luke warm, no sugar and still standing in a bowl of warm water. Another glass of hot water accompanied it, so I topped up the cup and drank it. Pretty repulsive was about the only way I could describe it, and so I decided at that moment that I'd stick to tea for the rest of the holiday.

The weather was about ten degrees Celsius, colder than Saigon and very foggy. The first stop of the day was at the Cham museum in Danang. It was pretty small and unimpressive, comprising mainly of stone statues, which combined Chinese and Indian culture. The Cham people were mainly Hindu. I looked at my watch, it was only 8.00am and I'd already done one museum.

The next stop was a marble craft centre. The workmen were outside with drills and chisels and the sound was utterly deafening yet none of them were wearing earplugs. What a place to work in. Then of course was the complimentary shop to walk around, and my goodness was it hard sell. "Did madam want this? Did madam want that? Was there anything madam liked?"......

I could have bought the whole shop, especially the huge statues and garden ornaments because everything was so beautifully crafted, but it was pretty expensive and the hard sell approach put me off. I quite liked some little statues of local musicians and decided that three would make a nice display at home. She wanted twenty dollars each, but after the usual bargaining, I got the three for thirty five dollars. I would normally have walked away because the pestering was beyond tolerance levels, but I liked these little figures and had learned from bitter experience that sometimes you can lose out by passing over something you desire, and then never see the like again. I told Jin about the over insistent nature of the sales girl, also sending him the message not to take me to any other places with such a hard sell attitude.

We arrived at Hoi An and what a beautiful town. There was a lot of Chinese influence and magnificently restored ancient buildings. House and shop walls were brightly coloured tawny, yellow and pink twinkling in the sunshine, and it was not difficult to imagine this lovely town a hub of activity as a major port in bygone days.

Colourful lanterns of deep fuchsia, ochre and brilliant orange hung across shop fronts and the entrances to mysterious little courtyards, many offering places for a snack or a beverage or just somewhere to rest your feet. The streets were bustling with character and fascination, however, it was all clearly done for tourists and there was a lot more pestering to buy things here than in the south. There were however some really good Kodak moments such as the old ladies with baskets and the fisherwomen, but if you took their picture they expected a tip. Their market was exceptional with a wide-ranging variety of fresh fruits, unusual vegetables, fish and meat, with the vibrant locals noisily bargaining as they bought their daily food. I paused to take in the colours and smells of all the exotic spices and wonderful flower displays.

I was taken to a silk factory where I was shown the live silk worms, through to boiling them, releasing their silk, winding it, weaving it, to embroidering it. I walked around their post-tour shop at such a pace that the sales girl had difficulty keeping up with me. I'd already been caught out once today.

We visited an old house where the family still made handicrafts, and again I walked around the shop at my new alarming pace. If Jin was expecting his cut from my purchases today he would be pretty disappointed.

By now it was 11.00am. The fog was clearing, the sun was breaking through and I felt like I'd already done a full day's sightseeing. We approached the Riverside Hotel which was just outside Hoi An, and I loved it as soon as we arrived. It was beautiful, open plan and traditionally styled. The accommodation was in buildings dotted around the gardens and I had a fantastic room which was spacious with wooden floors, and traditional furniture. After my exhausting morning there was time for some R&R by the pool.

Now that the fog had dissipated and the sun had come out, it was also very hot, so I read for an hour before going to the restaurant for lunch. Before I reached the restaurant, I slipped out of the main gates to stop by a laundry shack over the road from the hotel. Jin had told me that it was a lot cheaper than the hotel service. One of the problems with travelling light and only stopping a night here and there, was getting your laundry done at a price that wouldn't make it cheaper to just replace the garment.

After lunch, and a couple of Tiger beers which somewhat hit the spot, especially considering that I had been up since 4.00am, set me up nicely for an afternoon snooze. The temperature must have soared to mid to high eighties and I fell asleep quickly only awakening 3 hours later shivering and sniffly. Perhaps the sore throat of the last few days wasn't dust and fumes, but signs that a cold was on its way. It had now arrived. Feeling extremely lethargic, I staggered back to the room and popped a couple of Nurofen Cold and Flu tablets because I was determined that I was not going to go down with a cold. I rarely caught one, perhaps once every three to five years, but when I did, I stood a fifty percent chance of having it turn into a nasty bout of sinusitis, and I clearly didn't want this to happen in Vietnam.

This really was a gorgeous hotel in an extremely attractive location. Exceptionally peaceful and tranquil. I sat on the balcony of my room and gazed out over the paddy fields where I could see a few spots in the distance working. My view was partially blocked by a couple of banana trees, but the window through its branches allowed me glimpses of the water life as people rowed down the river periodically. Certainly an ambience for contemplation and musing.

When I reflect on the past, present and future, my mind inevitably drifts back to a near death experience about 7 years previously. I kept a meticulously up to date will. I wasn't morbid, but with my international job, and some potentially dangerous hobbies, I knew that accidents could happen. I held my private pilot's licence and whilst doing my final revision flight for my IMC rating (Instrument Meteorological Conditions), an aviation flight category that describes weather conditions that require pilots to fly primarily by reference to instruments as opposed to visual flying, we had an engine failure. We didn't have to do a forced landing because at about five hundred feet above ground the engine started again. It was a temporary fuel blockage. I was fine during the incident because all the emergency drills leapt to the forefront of my mind and occupied it one hundred percent, but I suffered post traumatic stress a few hours later. I was separated at the time, and when thinking about the incident over the weekend that followed I realised that had I died that day without a will, everything would had gone to my estranged husband who had run off with someone else. I'll be damned. The next working day I made an appointment to see a solicitor and had a will drawn up. Included in the will were letters for significant people. I suddenly thought of Mike, a penniless chap up north who I hadn't seen for 6 years, the person who rekindled a childhood interest in the outdoors with abseiling, rock climbing, kayaking, camping etc through an outward bounds organisation. He had probably forgotten me. Bet my name wouldn't even ring a bell, but when I lived in Cheshire he had had a huge impact on my love of the outdoors. Yes, there was a letter for him.

I considered this holiday and realised that so far I loved it and that I was extremely glad that I had booked it, even though at the time it was a bit of a comfort spend. Again, I was enthused that I was not in a group. By being alone it proved to me that I was largely happy with myself and my own company. I found it hard to write the words to describe how I was feeling at that very moment sitting on the balcony watching the sun go down. At peace, content, happy, bubbly, cheeky, powerful, strong, loving, gentle, invincible even. Whatever the words, I was feeling great, absolutely great.

I heard the twanging of a musical instrument in the distance, and my mind drifted back to my own musical ambitions. It was something I'd parked to give thought to whilst I was away. I guess in summary, I just wanted to play more and more, and preferably with other musicians. I'd found a regular jazz jam session six months ago in a place I affectionately called the Scout Hut, and it was like finding a goldmine. Although I didn't believe in fate per se, I found it at exactly the time I wanted and needed to, and the disciplines I learnt there were spot on in advance of my next stage of development. However, I still saw Scout Hut as a stepping stone to "something else," but I couldn't quite put my finger on what that "something else" was. At Scout Hut, we never "worked on" pieces, we just played number after number after number and although my comping (backing) skills had come on in leaps and bounds, I needed to find something where I could work on playing the melody and improvising. At Scout Hut, the solos were always given to the horns or keys, but never the accordion.

I had tried to start the ICI jazz band, however there just wasn't the commitment from the other members I recruited, so frequently we would have to cancel jam sessions at short notice when there was just me and one other musician turning up. Even I had to admit that frankly, just an accordion and drums duo didn't make a great sound.

The biggest issue for me was time. I already practiced a lot, but I could do with even more time. Music over the previous 12 months had become my main interest, passion and focus, and so I decided that I must make a conscious effort to divest myself of less interesting pursuits in the New Year to free up more time for music. I was stuck with various village commitments for a few months more, but then I would divest myself of them and after that must, must,

must learn to say NO! I found myself agreeing to help out a friend in the New Year before I came away, with the planning of a large murder mystery evening they were pulling together, where you had half a dozen actors mingling with the rest of the people, and only the actors knew who were the actors. They were missing a female part, the lead, would I help them out? The word "yes" was out of my mouth before I even had time to form it, let alone engage my brain. Didn't I have enough on my plate already? I generally didn't make New Year Resolutions, however my "motto" for 2004 would be "Just say No, in two oh four", and then I could really push forward with my music.

I would like to get some more solo gigs, but had a preference for playing with others. It's like a drug, once you've had a taste of it, you're addicted. I loved all the playing with others experienced at Scout Hut and a few socials when Stephen had allowed me to sit in with his band for a few numbers, and I wanted more. There was a feeling of belonging, being part of something, rather than an outsider looking in. Creating something where the sum of the parts was definitely greater than the whole. It would be interesting in 12 months time to see where I'm at musically. Yes, to be reviewed next holiday.....

I was taking weekly accordion lessons with a surly second generation Hungarian called Lev, short for Levente. He lived in a rundown terraced house with the proverbial dishes stacked up in the kitchen and wiffy sleeping bags on the settee for friends who had crashed out at short notice. It wasn't unusual for me to have to wait 5 minutes whilst he cleared a path from the living room door through piles of music, records and clothes to the chair where I'd be seated for my lesson. From the first lesson he would shout and rant at me if I played a wrong note or used the wrong finger. Initially I put up with it because he was the only teacher I could find within driving distance, however I rapidly realised that he was a stunningly gifted musician albeit with a huge second generation chip on his shoulder. I did try one other chap, but he was exactly the opposite and would say everything sounded fine, when it clearly didn't and so on balance I preferred the strict tutoring of Lev, because I was at least learning something, even if I had to put up with his Hungarian tantrums. After six months he didn't shout at me too much, but still picked on me from time to time, especially over jazz, and especially when a jazz intonation or rhythm crept into some of my homework pieces, none of which were jazz. He was a classical accordion perfectionist, but some of the classical techniques were not suitable for jazz. Lev could obviously play them all, but he was very strict about me learning how to play "classically" first before expanding into other genres. However, it's fair to say that staccato Um-cha-cha in the bass, which was perfect for French Musette, just didn't sound right in jazz.

Whether it was subconsciously recalling piles of unwashed clothes in Lev's living room or my built in mental alarm clock, I was jolted back to the moment when I realised that it was time to collect my laundry, which turned out to be a fraction of the hotel price. The laundry woman's dog peed on my foot, and I was wearing open sandals. She was ever so apologetic and I said that there was no problem, but I could see that she was uncomfortable about it. Although she didn't understand me, I waved my hands as I said again that it really wasn't a problem as I could very easily wash my feet and sandals back at the hotel. However I felt uncomfortable because she was uncomfortable.

I returned to the hotel, washed my feet and sandals, dressed for dinner and by 8.00pm I was sitting in the Riverside restaurant. A Vietnamese group was playing in the background, some of it was haunting and highly emotionally charged Chinese music on their various local instruments. Some was like Kitaro's type of music. Kitaro was a new age Japanese composer whose tunes stay in your head for days and years. They were also playing some classics, such as Ave Maria. My table was looking out over the river and at the other side I could see little beacons flickering in the dark. A boat was drifting by the restaurant putting lighted Chinese lanterns into the river to float past the hotel. It was a truly poignant and romantic experience and I was feeling in top notch, sitting alone in an exquisite restaurant in a stunning location on Christmas Eve, watching Chinese lanterns, hundreds of them, slowly wend their way down the river.

OK, let's be honest, I'd rather have been sitting there with "someone special" sharing that unique experience than sitting alone, but importantly, it did not negatively impact me in the least. I remained present with the moment and almost felt honoured to be allowed to experience this Christmas Eve pageant.

It was only five minutes walk back to my building in the gardens, and the night was so calm that only the warble of the cicadas was heard. I saw the occasional flicker of a Chinese lantern still floating down the river in the distance and decided at that moment that I was going to mark this evening as the best ever Christmas Eve.

Marble Mountains and Hue – Christmas Day

It was Christmas day, but it didn't feel like it. Great, that's exactly what I wanted. I had a very bad night's sleep with just a couple of hours here and there and lots of coughing and sneezing. Yes, I had a streaming cold. I'd finished all of my cough medicine so needed to get some more. I had breakfast then packed up ready to move on. My suitcase seemed incredibly full, yet I hadn't bought that much stuff and I had even offloaded a couple of holiday trash books at the last hotel.

Before I left the hotel, I went back over to the laundry woman and gave her some pens for her kids. Whenever I travel to a developing or relatively poor country, I always take a box of 100 biros with me as stationery is generally in short supply in such countries and with families having to provide their own paper and pens for school, some just haven't got the money to do so. Furthermore they don't take up much room in a suitcase and are relatively light to carry around with you. Also when coming across beggars, I'd rather give a begging child a pen than money, not that I'd seen any beggars here. I recalled my first trip to India many years ago when the tour guide advised us against giving money to the begging children however imploring and persistent they were, for the simple reason that the child rarely got the money as it went straight to the pimp. We were told that if we wanted to give money, then it was best to purchase something even if it went in the hotel bin as this was at least contributing to the economy. For children, sweets or pens always went down a treat, and wouldn't be taken off them. I also use biro pens as "gifts", which was the purpose on this occasion of going back to see the laundry woman and then she would know that I had forgiven her dog for peeing on my foot. She was absolutely delighted, and we swapped a few sentences in sign language.

We set off and I was sneezing and sniffling and my nose being rather akin to a waterfall. I'd never known it to run so constantly. It really was like that proverbial tap that had been left on. Jin asked if I need to see a doctor. I told him that this wasn't necessary, but I wouldn't mind stopping at a pharmacy and getting something to at least dry up the nose and calm down the cough, so we stopped in the next village. Even though it was Christmas Day all the shops were open. I bought another bottle of cough mixture and asked Jin to explain to the pharmacist that my nose was pouring and I wanted something to dry it up. Ideally I was after something like Contac 400, but the pharmacist just shook her head as she hadn't heard of it before. I explained to Jin that I wanted something similar. The pharmacist explained via Jin that she didn't have one tablet to dry up a cold, but could make up a concoction for me. She emptied various jars with different shapes, sizes and colours of pills, counted some out and made three little piles, each with six tablets. Each group of six tablets she put in a tiny plastic bag. My dosage. I was to take all three packs over the next twenty four hours. I was somewhat reluctant to take a load of pills I knew nothing about, in a country I didn't know, given to me in a language I couldn't speak, but as I really didn't want the cold to spoil the holiday I trusted to fate and Vietnamese pharmacology and took the contents of the first packet. I told Jin at the same time, that if I collapsed, he was to show the doctor at the hospital one of the remaining packets so they'd know what I'd taken. He laughed. He thought I was joking.

Although it was Christmas Day, not only were the shops open but the kids were also going to school. A large proportion of Vietnamese are atheist or practice indigenous religions worshiping local spirits, gods and mother goddesses, however the main religion is Buddhism, and less than ten percent are Christian, hence the twenty fifth of December was just a normal day.

I hadn't really taken to Jin as I had to Jung. Apart from the fact that he had terminal body odour, he had an unfortunate manner about him. He was constantly telling me that he was number one in his English class, number one in his tourism diploma class, knew lots of highly placed people, strongly believed in imparting his knowledge to others and that he looked after and looked out for his family and friends. It was not done in a boastful arrogant way but more like a Uriah Heap type person, humble but brilliant. This manner irked after a while. He worked his way up from the bottom starting as a tea boy selling tea to people waiting to cross on a ferry. Then when he'd made enough money at this, he upgraded to a candy boy, then a cigarette boy and eventually earned enough money to buy a bicycle. He learned how to take bicycles apart and put them back together again then went into business with his father repairing cycles. During his 3 years conscription he learned engineering and after that went to college to learn English. I genuinely and truly admired him for his entrepreneurial ventures, tenaciousness, diligence and perseverance, but I still didn't take to him.

He explained a little more about the education system. You had to have a certain number of points to be able to go to University. Some of these were based on personal ability, whilst others were based on seemingly spurious criteria such as whether your father was a member of the communist party or not.

The weather was much cooler than in the south, probably around fifty five degrees with drizzle. The first stop was at the Marble Mountains. There were five of these but we only climbed one. It was pretty hard work on the legs as every step was about a foot high, and there were two hundred and fifty of them. Half way up there was a Chinese temple and a vista point. Jin started talking to a group of school kids on an outing. They gathered around me and one of them asked their teacher to ask Jin to ask me if they could have their photo taken with me. I said yes, no problem, and then they all become giggly and excited, pushing and shoving to see who was going to be closest to me. As I left them, there was a loud chorus of "good-byes" ringing in my ears.

There was also a cave to visit up this mountain, with Buddhist icons to worship. There were two stalactites, although one had dried up and was no longer forming. The other, still dripping, was supposed to bring you good luck if you touch it. I touched it. Perhaps my nose would stop dripping now.

The next stop in Danang was Jin's house. He needed to pick something up and asked if I'd like to see inside. Yes, of course. It was not every day you got to see the inside of a Vietnamese house. I stepped straight into the living room. It was about fifteen feet square and in it were three motorbikes (his and his two brothers who lived with him), a little table with some plastic chairs around it, a "put-me-up" bed where one of his brothers slept and several much cluttered shelves. There was a tiny kitchenette area in one corner with a small chipped enamel sink and a small Baby Belling type cooker. Jin apparently had a room at the back and his other brother had one upstairs. What with three young men living in the house it wasn't the tidiest or cleanest I'd ever seen. It was really only one step up from a hovel, but he was clearly very proud of it.

We then set off for Hue, going past China Beach where the Americans first landed, then up into the mountains via a precarious narrow hair-pinned bend road. The scenery was very different to the south with fewer trees, more moorland and a rocky landscape. We stopped at the top for a comfort break and a cup of tea. Three young ladies tried to sell their wares. One was selling a little kit of mixed Tiger Balm products. Tiger Balm is made from a secret herbal formulation that dates back to the times of the Chinese emperors and has a strong odour of menthol and camphor. It is believed to cure many ailments, for example it can be used as an anti-inflammatory on practically any part of the body, to relieve muscle aches, for colds and flu either rubbed under the nose or dropped in hot water to breath in the vapours, treat headaches, to stop mosquito bites from itching and even to treat minor burns. I had tried some in the dim and distant past, though couldn't recall exactly when or what for, but did have positive memories of its medicinal claims, so I decided to get some as my nose was red raw from blowing and sneezing. Another lady persuaded me to buy some postcards taken from various vantage points up the road. The third one was selling bracelets. I didn't really want one but as they were only the equivalent of ninety pence I got one to keep them all happy, as I couldn't buy from two and not the third. Then remembering the India tale of putting money into their economy, I bought three more bracelets. The ladies were all very friendly and chatty and the bracelet woman spoke a little English. Most Vietnamese didn't speak any English, so my sign language was progressing very well. I also gave out some more biros.

Most of the public toilets I'd come across were clean but a little shabby. The one on the top of this mountain was a squat type, but without an obvious hole. Two breeze blocks were in place for your feet, you then squatted and basically peed on the tiles then used a small bucket in a water tank to swill down the floor to a minute drainage hole in the corner. I emphasise "minute" drainage hole as thank God I only needed a pee. Toilets outside the hotels were like their miniature plastic chairs that are made for Vietnamese sized people. You'd go to sit on the loo then drop a further 6 inches lower than you'd expect.

As we progressed on our journey and had just driven past three stray dogs, I asked Jin whether there was any truth in the fact that the Vietnamese ate dog.

"Well, I guess there is some truth in it," he replied "the Vietnamese do still eat dog, but it's only common amongst poor families in rural areas where they catch wild dogs. I've never eaten it and I don't think my friends have. You don't see it on menus in restaurants. We are not like Korea you know, where they have dog farms for mass production, and you'd actually see it on restaurant menus."

I thought that Korea won't be top of my list of countries to visit in the future, as dogs have always been my surrogate children, and the thought of eating one was revolting and akin to cannibalism. I recalled being taken to Shanghai Zoo during a business trip, specifically to show off their pandas, however en-route to their enclosure, we passed a row of cages exhibiting dog breeds from around the world, including a Lassie Rough Collie, the same as my dog. It had broken my heart to see them, even though there was no logical reason to be more concerned about dogs being locked up than monkeys.

I wasn't convinced that the pharmacist had understood my tablet request or whether Jin misunderstood me before translating, but since taking the tablets my nose had started running like an open tap at full flow. I guess that somewhere in the translations, running nose had become blocked nose, so I'd been given a cocktail of decongestants. I used the recently purchased Tiger Balm to calm down my sore red muzzle. It had a strong eucalyptus smell, so also successfully blocked out Jin's body odour.

We arrived at Hue and went straight to the restaurant for lunch. It was certainly a Christmas lunch with a difference. All the dishes were served in the most stunning manner with carved vegetables and fruits. The locals must have found it highly amusing that I photographed each dish as it arrived. However, it was not every day that I was served a Christmas banquet like this.

After lunch, which lasted two and half hours, which is some going when you are eating alone, it was on to the hotel where I gave Joe a Christmas phone call. He'd had a row with Penny (another one!) so was spending Christmas Day alone. I was the only person who had called him to wish him Happy Christmas.

I went for a brief walk to see what was out and about in Hue. It was quite a large town, circa one hundred thousand inhabitants. The hotel was by the Perfume River but there wasn't much to see around it so I walked down to the nearest bridge that crossed the river, strolled along the bank on the other side then came back over the second bridge. I passed a couple of shops so stocked up on film, coffee and milk and I also bought some biscuits. As I had had a mammoth late lunch I was envisaging that I wouldn't eat that evening, but needed something in case I got the munchies.

Back in the hotel I had a couple of beers and caught up with the diary. The hotel was French colonial in style, not a dissimilar feel to Raffles in Singapore, however there was little ambience, unlike the hotel in Can Tho. I attempted to make a cup of coffee. I'd bought it from a shop where they didn't speak English. After much sign language concerning ground down coffee beans to powder, I'd bought a small packet of what looked like instant coffee. But it wasn't, it was filter coffee, so the one cup I attempted to make was definitely undrinkable, unless of course you like floaters in your coffee. At this point I realised that I was just destined not to get a decent cup of coffee during the holiday, which was a good excuse to go down to the hotel bar for a drink.

Over a beer I struck up a conversation with a New Zealand girl who had spent nearly two years travelling around Asia back packing with friends. She was staying in bed and breakfast accommodation but needed a plate of "decent plain" food as she was allergic to almost all spices, hence visiting my hotel. It must have been a nightmare for her travelling around Asia for that length of time effectively allergic to all foods on offer. She told me that she bumps into people all the time and strikes up conversations with fellow travellers. Last night she was in a local bar where they met other travellers and despite good intentions ended up clubbing, getting pissed and returning to the bed and breakfast in the early hours of the morning. She was planning to meet up with them again for another session that evening and asked whether I'd like to join them. As it was my idea of an evening in hell, I used my cold as a polite excuse and declined the invitation.

Back in the room I decided that I was not taking the third packet of multi coloured pills as I was sure by now they were decongestants rather than what I wanted – the opposite, so instead, I dosed up on cough mixture and called it a night.

Hue and Temples – Boxing Day

Another dreadful night's sleep, but I felt a little better cold wise than I did the day before. I didn't need the alarm clock as there was drilling directly above my head. No, it wasn't a hangover from the couple of glasses of Vietnamese wine I'd had the previous evening, but as I found out later, they were adding an additional floor to the hotel.

It was chucking it down with rain, but it wasn't cold. Having decided that I'd probably put on loads of weight so far this holiday because of the delectable food in gigantic portions, I restricted myself to a plate of fresh local fruits for breakfast.

The first stop of the day was a river ride on the Perfume River, so called because of the fragrant smell during the flowering season. It was not the flowering season, and it was difficult to imagine this murky brown water smelling of anything other than, well, murky brown water. I had my own boat again, however there wasn't as much to see as there was in the Mekong, though there wasn't much to see anyway because of the rain.

We'd hardly left the shore when out came the silk tapestries, wooden carvings and silk clothes. I rolled my eyes at Jin. He knew exactly what I meant because the previous day I had told him straight out that I didn't like the "hard sell" approach and that if I'm given the opportunity to browse by myself with minimal pestering, there was a greater likelihood I may buy something. As I know that guides are on commission, a smart guide would ensure that my future shopping experiences were exactly tailored to my preferences to supplement their income. Jin wasn't that smart.

The boat owner had two kids, so more biro pens were distributed. I looked through the silk tapestries and found 3 small ones that would make a nice collection. I also bought a wooden figure for Joe. I was then shown how to wear one of their silk suits. The top was straightforward, but the culottes were somewhat more complicated. They were trousers without side seams. You fastened them around your waist, then lifted up the legs and tied a second ream of material around the waist, thereby covering the backside. The easiest way to describe them was as a close fitting nappy with long legs.

They had a beautiful Kingfisher blue suit, but not in my size. Their red one was, but I didn't wear red. I tried on a green one with a pattern which was very nice, but I couldn't wear it back home, not even as fancy dress. I bought a black silk one that would be suitable for business evening do's. It cost the equivalent of six pounds.

We were only in the boat for about half an hour before we disembarked to see the Thien Mu Pagoda and Tomb. It was unfortunate that it was still raining and also that they were starting to renovate the pagoda and tomb, so they were cocooned in scaffolding. Both had been damaged during the American war, and they still had a long way to go with the restoration.

Also at this complex was the car of Thich Quang Duc. He was a Vietnamese Mahayana Buddhist monk who burned himself to death at a busy Saigon road junction on 11th June 1963. He was protesting against the persecution of Buddhists by the South

Vietnamese government led by Ngo Dinh Diem. Photos of his self-immolation were circulated widely across the world and brought attention to the policies of the Diem government. John F Kennedy was reported to have said *"No news picture in history had generated so much emotion around the world as that one."* After Duc's death, his body was re-cremated, but despite two burnings his heart had remained intact, and has since been revered as a holy relic, standing for compassion.

"Today" said Jin a little pompously "I'm going to explain how the Vietnamese people are very superstitious. We will see symbols everywhere, usually meaning vitality or longevity or prosperity or fertility or happiness or......" his voice trailed off as he ran out of omens, then after a few minutes he had composed himself and continued.

"It is very complicated because many symbols have duplicate meanings."

"So in summary, does that mean they all pretty much mean good health and a long life?" I asked, trying not to sound too sceptical. Thankfully Jin didn't pick up on my intonation and continued.

"Numbers. It's all about numbers. They are the key to everything."

Jin would point out trucks with a registration plate including the number five.

"Very lucky - number five," he would say gravely. Then a number nine, and it wasn't long before I realised that all numbers were lucky in one way or the other.

Three was lucky because it represented heaven, earth and humanity. Five was lucky because it represented the five elements (hence the five Marble Mountains were lucky). Four was lucky because it represented the seasons. Seven was lucky because of the seven Buddhist stages to Nirvana. Nine was lucky because of five plus four. Eight was lucky because of five plus three. And so on.....

As we walked around the buildings Jin would say "Seven steps – very lucky". "Three roofs – very lucky." or "Four statues – very lucky"......

Throughout the rest of the day I visited 3 tombs from the Nguyen dynasty. The first one was Tu Duc (1848 – 1883). It was set in lovely countryside and had a little pavilion overlooking an artificial island where the emperor used to sit and write poetry. It was believed that he had had up to five hundred concubines in addition to his wife. Women, on the other hand could only have one partner, and if found to be unfaithful would be executed.

The second tomb was that of Minh Mang, the second emperor of this particular dynasty from 1791 to 1841. Again it was set in beautiful surroundings. The stone warriors guarding his tomb were shorter than one would expect to find, however they were specifically built this way as this particular emperor was very short and they couldn't have had the warriors towering over him. The stone warriors were not dissimilar in style to those in Xian, China. The Nguyen dynasty tombs generally followed a similar design. There was a front gate that had only ever been used once, and that was to take the emperors body through, after which it would have been sealed never to be opened again. Then there was a pavilion with a tombstone standing upright, about ten feet tall with the story of the life of the emperor inscribed on it. Following in a straight line from the gate through the pavilion you came to the temple, a very ornate affair made from lacquered wood and lots of gold filigree work, then on from that would be the tomb. However not all emperors were actually buried in the tombs. Some would be buried deep in a hillside with their treasures and valuables some meters away to protect their whereabouts from grave hunters. At this particular tomb it was rumoured that a long passageway was burrowed into the hillside behind to make the tomb and then the peasants who had built it had been executed so that they couldn't reveal its location.

The last tomb was that of Khai Dink (1916 – 1925) the penultimate emperor in Vietnam and an extremely unpopular leader, who was perceived by his subjects as nothing more than a salaried employee of the French. Its architecture was a combination of oriental and occidental. It was grotesquely ornate, with one hundred steps leading up to it, and enamelled mosaics and gold everywhere. Khai Dink, who only "ruled" for nine years, was effectively a puppet emperor as the French were ruling at the time. He chose the spot for his tomb, which took eleven years to build and was finished long after his death. He only lived to forty, dying of tuberculosis. The tomb was very beautiful, but incredibly arrogant.

The day also included a visit to the Imperial Citadel. This was built very much along the same lines as The Forbidden City in Beijing. The Chinese emperor at the time wouldn't allow an exact replica to be built, especially not allowing the same five entrance passageways into the complex, so the Vietnamese emperor only built three visible from the outside, but added two additional entrances which could only be seen from within. Unfortunately there were very few buildings still standing within the complex thanks to B52 bombers. However, those still standing were being painstakingly restored to their former glory, though at the time of my visit, only a couple had been completed.

It was a real shame about the weather that day because the Imperial Citadel and the tombs would have looked quite stunning on a dry sunny day especially because of their setting at the foot of mountains. Unfortunately that day they could only be seen through the rain and fog. I guess it saved me a lot of film.

We passed numerous roadside shop-shacks on the way back to Hue, including one where they made incense sticks. As I had never seen how these were made I asked Jin to stop so that I could watch. Little girls aged about six to twelve were making them. They wound a sticky dough of aromatic biotic materials onto thin bamboo sticks then rolled them. They were then dipped into dye to colour them. I bought a few multi coloured packs for Joe.

In total contrast to the incense shacks, there were also men making marble statues by the roadside. The noise from the drilling and chipping was deafening, and you could taste the dust in the air.

Most of them were wearing face masks to minimize the inhalation of the particles, but none were wearing ear muffles.

I got back to the hotel at around 4.00pm and went for a little walk, heading in a different direction to the day before. I passed lots of small local shops with no intention of buying anything, and just letting the Vietnamese culture seep into every pore. I wanted to take in the ambience and soak up the local atmosphere, however, I was constantly pestered by cycle rickshaws or motor bikers, crying out,

"City tour, city tour. One hour. Good price."

I waved "no" as I kept on walking but they continued to pester me until I was out of earshot. I wouldn't go on a cycle rickshaw out of principal. There was no way I'd have another human being pedal me around, especially one half the size of myself. And there was no way I was getting on the back of a bike. I remembered that many years ago when I was fresh out of university, worldly unwise, naive and earning my first pittance salary, that I "did" Italy on the cheap. Arriving in Venice, my boyfriend and I were persuaded by a young student earning holiday money, to take a gondola at a "very cheap price." The problem with a gondola was that once you were in it, you can't get out until it docks again, so we not only saw every waterway of Venice, despite our protestations that we just wanted to go straight to St. Marks Square, but we also took an unwanted trip out to Murano island to visit the glass blowing factory and surprise, surprise its linked gift shop. The eventual arrival in St. Marks Square was marred by an argument between the gondolier and ourselves over the cost of the journey, with the young lad, in a foul mood because we didn't make any purchases at the glass shop, screeching at the top of his voice in English "These tourists are trying to rip me off." We eventually calmed him down by giving him what little cash we had, a packet of tobacco and twenty Marlboro. So no, I was not going to get on the back of a motorbike with an unknown itinerary or destination. I smiled brightly as I said "no" and carried on without slowing, but after the hundredth pester, I muttered to myself "oh just fuck off".

Back at the hotel, I had a couple of non-alcoholic cocktails and reserved a table for dinner in the garden. I made a quick phone call to Joe to check that he was okay, and he was still a bit wobbly with all the rowing with his girlfriend, but at least they were speaking again. I then picked up my e-mails before dinner and there were several more Christmas wishes.

In my room I had a couple of hours to kill before dinner, so I got my "Vietnam CDs" out, ones I had prepared for the holiday which were a compilation of all the jazz and blues songs I could play, and also the little plastic keyboard. I sat and played along, trying some improvisations as I went. I wasn't sure how much value this exercise had, except that it made me pick out the key to fluff along without printed music, which was good exercise for playing by ear. I guess after one session the usefulness of the holiday keyboard was unproven, but I did play for almost two hours.

I made the effort to dress for dinner, the pink Indian outfit again. I felt terrific, I looked pretty great and I had a marvellous dinner. I was developing a different outlook to travelling alone than I used to have. Yes, people did look at me sitting by myself with only a book or my diary to keep me company. I'd always interpreted these sideways glances as "pity" or simply rudeness in staring. That night I was above all that, and I saw the looks as totally different, envy, longing, admiration. As I made my way around the buffet carts I felt as if I was gliding, head high, back straight. I adored this holiday, and I loved myself.

Arrival in Hanoi - 27th December

If I thought I hadn't been sleeping well the last few nights, then the next night was the night in hell. I just couldn't get to sleep and switch my brain off. I tried listening to soft music; it didn't work. I tried meditation; it didn't work. I took a sleeping tablet; it didn't work. I took a second: it didn't work. I think my brain was just zinging from all the amazing places I'd visited and people I'd met, and that it needed night time to catalogue it all.

I drifted off to sleep around 3.30am. At 7.15am I was awoken abruptly by the banging on the ceiling, the hotel extension. I had a sense of humour failure and called reception saying that it was unacceptable to start work so early. They apologised and said they would ask the workmen to stop. I told them that the damage was done as I was now wide awake. I looked like shit with huge bags under my eyes and a generally drawn look, indicating that I'd had about a nano second of reasonable sleep. I filled in the guest relations questionnaire and dropped it off at reception on the way to breakfast.

My pick up was at 12.00 noon. It was belting down with rain and the hotel only had a small foyer area to sit in, so I stayed in the room, listened to music and read. I was shattered but just couldn't go back to sleep, and the banging on the roof continued unabated. I checked out at 11.30am. After paying the bill the cashier told me that they forgot to charge me commission on the cheques I cashed last night and that I had to pay the extra now. Her attitude was brusque and surly. She'd seen the questionnaire I had completed and couldn't understand why I was complaining about the noise so I lifted my sunglasses and showed her the slits I had as eyes. She just shrugged. I paid my additional two dollars commission begrudgingly, using my Visa card just to be awkward and then waited for Jin to pick me up.

He arrived beaming and asked if I liked the hotel. I relayed my tale of the noise and surly service. He asked if I wanted a refund and I said no, but I did want him to report my dissatisfaction to his office so that they could use an alternative hotel to prevent future guests sleeping in the middle of a building site. The hotel gave me a packed lunch and then we were off to the airport for my flight to Hanoi.

Hue airport was miniscule, consisting of only one small brick building, although they were building a new terminal next to it. I said farewell to Jin and his driver then settled down to eat my packed lunch outside. It consisted of a greasy piece of turkey, a bread roll, a squidgy tomato, a chunk of wizened cucumber and an orange. Clearly the hotel had spent a lot of time throwing this together. I fed the rubbish bin.

There was a dark skinned surly policeman guarding the door to the airport. He kept slapping his baton into his hand as if he was expecting a riot to break out, despite this looking like the sort of airport that had one flight a week. He looked menacing and superior and I wouldn't want to have crossed him.

I was feeling very dopey and tired, probably due to a combination of lack of accumulated sleep and sleeping tablets taken too late, or rather too early in the morning. The cold was now turning into sinusitis, and my forehead felt like it was in a vice. Great! I could now do with a decongestant and wished I hadn't thrown away the last packet of multi-coloured pills.

The flight to Hanoi was only an hour, but my ears clogged up with the pressure and didn't pop again. So I arrived in Hanoi tired, dopey, thick headed and hardly able to hear.

Whin greeted me at the airport. She was a petite, attractive Vietnamese girl who could have been any age between nineteen and thirty five. The drive to the hotel took around an hour. Hanoi was more modern in comparison to the rest of Vietnam, but not "modern" by western standards. There was a strong French architectural influence and many houses were painted in very bright colours. Hotel Sofitel was another large anonymous business type hotel, teeming with Japanese people. My room was small in comparison with previous rooms, but it was comfortable and at the end of a corridor, so hopefully quiet.

It was around 4.00pm so I stayed in my room and read one of my holiday books, Lovely Bones by Alice Seabold, which turned out to be an excellent read. I made a mental note that I would read other novels by her when I got home.

I had an early dinner, and checked my e-mails en-route to the restaurant. I sent one to Joe telling him that I may not phone again, as the call in the last hotel cost forty pounds and I wasn't getting a signal on my mobile. I said that I hoped things were settling down for him on the woman front and that at the very least, things were "calmer". I opted for the cheaper, twelve dollar buffet restaurant and got a quiet table in the corner. However I was soon surrounded by a Japanese family with about a million kids ranging from a baby who bawled all the way through the meal to the young siblings who thought it was a great idea to play tag around the tables. Zero parental control or discipline. I think my "noise" tolerance level just gets lower as I get older.

With the meal finished, and having eaten somewhat faster than usual to escape the mayhem surrounding me, I retired around 9.00pm, got into bed, fell asleep immediately and had the best night's sleep I'd had in weeks.

Hanoi tour - 28th December

Wow! A decent night's sleep despite my head still feeling full of concrete, but I was definitely on the mend. The medical problem today was that I was now running low on tampons. Erm, this could be interesting.

I took a light breakfast then met Whin for my tour around Hanoi City.

The first stop was a visit to Uncle Ho's mausoleum. Ho Chi Minh was even now referred to as Uncle Ho by everyone and was still loved and revered by the Vietnamese. You were not allowed to take cameras or bags into the mausoleum, so Whin held mine. You then had to walk through an X-ray machine in single file. About 20 of us formed a queue and were then escorted by a soldier to the mausoleum. He was marching and we suddenly found ourselves falling in step subconsciously. Once inside you were not allowed to talk and a guard told the girl in front of me to take her hands out of her pockets and show respect. We were then filed through a darkened room with Uncle Ho lying in state in the centre. His face and hands were lit up by soft lighting. It was a very peaceful scene although it did make my flesh tingle a little seeing him lying there.

There is a famous black and white photo showing Uncle Ho meeting Chairman Mao. I had now seen both of these people. Uncle Ho looked better preserved than Mao as I recalled him as looking like a Madame Tussaud waxwork, not a real person. Uncle Ho looked real.

Behind the mausoleum was a large French palace, but Ho had refused to live in it preferring a simpler lifestyle so he had opted to live in the garden. Firstly in a brick building and then in 1958 moved to an unpretentious stilt hut made from wood. You could look into the rooms and they were indeed very minimalistic. There were lots of trees in the garden. Ho liked trees so visitors used to bring them for him as gifts. There was also a large lake that he used to run around every morning. The lake was filled with Koi carp, many of which would have been there in Ho's day. Even now they were occasionally given away as a gift to visiting dignitaries as a present from Uncle Ho. All in all it was a lovely tranquil setting and I imagined that it would be especially beautiful in spring when all the flowers were in bloom.

The next expedition was to a museum, which explained the wars up to the expulsion of the French. One interesting military strategy was to put wooden stakes in the riverbed when the tide was low, then when the French ships came in during high tide, the stakes would rip the bottoms out of their boats.

The third outing of the morning was to the first university of Vietnam, built in 1077 and it was a seat of learning according to Confucius and was originally called the Palace of Literacy. Tombstones commemorating the great teachers were mounted on the backs of stone turtles to carry them safely and slowly to the next world. Many of the turtles heads were worn smooth by locals touching them for good luck and wisdom. The place had an ambience of knowledge about it and all the buildings had a strong Chinese influence.

I was then taken to a restaurant for lunch, although Whin left me as she said she had some shopping to do and would grab something to eat whilst she was out.. There was just one other couple in the restaurant. The woman was American, brash and spoke at decibels beyond my comfort zone, yak yak yak. When they left I looked at the staff and using my hands as mouths like a glove puppet mimicked "yak yak yak" and they all laughed. They had found her loud as well.

After lunch we went to a museum displaying artefacts from the Bronze Age, which held little interest for me. I told Whin discreetly that I needed to buy some sanitary protection and so could we stop off at an appropriate shop. We stopped in a main road and went into one of the shack shops with the frontage straight onto the street. Whin asked the assistant for me and the assistant handed over a packet of pads. I said to Whin that I actually wanted tampons. She didn't understand me, so again very discreetly, I plucked one out my back pack and turned to the wall showing it to her in cupped hands. She took it off me and held it up in the air examining it as she told me that she'd never seen one of these before and you probably wouldn't be able to get them in Vietnam. I positively squirmed with embarrassment as we were in a busy thoroughfare. I just couldn't imagine this happening in England.

I was however in luck as during our walk we passed a pharmacy that was more modern than the usual apothecary shops I had seen and they sold tampons, so I was saved.

Then to the Jade temple on Turtle Island which we accessed via a Chinese wooden red bridge. Hanoi had loads of lakes, which gave it a wide, airy feel rather than the usual claustrophobic big city feel. Apparently there were still giant turtles in the lake, however they rarely surfaced during the winter so I was unlikely to see any. The weather was much cooler in Hanoi and I had now switched since arriving to chinos rather than shorts. I had had to wear trousers anyway for my visit to Ho's mausoleum. It was still warm enough for me to wear a polo shirt, but the locals were all wrapped up in woolly jumpers and winter coats.

The final activity of the day was a stroll through the old quarter. There were bustling, relatively narrow streets with shops selling everything you could imagine, and more. Each street was called Hung xxx – the xxx being what they sold. So Paper Street sold paper products, Silver Street sold silver products and so on. Although it was a tourist attraction because of the quaintness of the streets and the bustling ambience, it was actually where the locals did most of their shopping. In the fresh produce area there were also little stalls down the centre of the road selling food and drink. We stopped for a snack and Whin bought me a drink of lotus seed and coconut. Not especially tasty but we sat on the little benches with the locals so it was worth it for the experience.

We passed shops in Tin Street that sold little ovens for burning money. Yes, you are reading correctly, burning money. When someone died, their money was burnt as an offering. However, this practice was polluting the air when it was burnt on open fires, so people now bought these little ovens to burn the money in as an alternative.

We should have stopped at another temple on the way back to the hotel, however it was closed for refurbishment and I wasn't especially disappointed as I'd seen enough Chinese temples in the last 10 days to last me a lifetime.

Back at the hotel Whin said that she would show me on a map where a good restaurant was, so I asked at reception for a city map. They sent me to the business centre where I had to pay one dollar for it. Ok, it was only a dollar, but I was gob smacked as it was the first time I'd ever had to pay anywhere in the world for a basic city map at a hotel. Still I bought one.

My hotel room hadn't been made up, nor my laundry returned. This hotel was starting to irritate me. It was a huge, impersonal business hotel and you had to pay for every teeny-weeny bit of service, including the flimsy city maps. Although I wasn't expecting any emails I decided to log on and see if there was anything waiting, but their computer just wouldn't pick up AOL. I guess it was one of those days. Hanoi was the last section of the holiday. I had a day at Halong Bay the next day, then one day free, then home. Goodness knows what I'd find to do in Hanoi for a day, and the hotel didn't even have gardens where I could sit and read.

I preferred Southern Vietnam to the north, and if I was going to advise anyone on a holiday here, I'd recommend starting in the north and heading south rather than the other way round, so that the holiday finishes on an exceptional high. There was no single reason why I liked the south better but it was probably a combination of more friendly people, less tourism, less commercialism, more things to see, more authentic and more stunning scenery. Plus of course I had had an excellent guide with Jung who really brought the place alive for me.

I had a beer in the bar and the piped music in the background was playing Autumn Leaves and I felt a bit home-sick as this was one of the jazz numbers I played frequently. I missed my accordion, my house and Misty my twelve year old Rough Collie. I dreamt about Misty one night early in the holiday. She could talk and we sat down and had a real good chinwag like two best friends sharing our thoughts and feelings.

Halong Bay - 29th December

I had a brilliant night's sleep. Today was a journey up to the northeast, to Halong Bay. It was a long drive of about three hours so we stopped half way at a handicraft centre where disabled people made and sold crafts. They had the most gorgeous tapestries of silk embroidery. They made the one I that I had crafted back home look decidedly amateurish. They were a different type though, long stitch rather than cross stitch and I considered that I may try and make one when I got home.

They also sold jewellery with a variety of semi precious stones. For the last few days I'd had a hankering to buy myself a ring. A little peculiar as I'm not a jewellery person in the least, however, I wanted to buy myself a gift to represent how great I was feeling about myself, and as a ring was probably one of the most symbolic expressions of love, I had got it into my head to buy myself a ring. When I do wear jewellery, I like very simple and discreet pieces, and all the rings they were selling at this craft centre had stone clusters of a size way above my preference zone. There was one that quite took my fancy at two hundred dollars, but it was still a little ostentatious for my liking so I decided to keep looking. If I didn't find one in Vietnam, I could treat myself when I got home.

As we carried along the road, Whin suddenly said,

"Look – do you see those paddy fields with the little mausoleums in them?"

"Yes," I replied and then pointed "Look, there is another. What are they?"

"People are frequently buried in their rice fields. After 3 years they are dug up and then re-buried in a new coffin. During these 3 years the family is in mourning. No one in the family can marry during this period, and people may wear white head bands (à la kamikaze) when they go to the temple to pray, to physically show that they are in a mourning period. After the second coffin has been buried that marks the end of mourning, although most families continue to pay their respects to the dead in the middle of each lunar period. So the little mausoleums are where they are first buried."

"They just look a little weird stuck in the middle of the field like that," I replied. "Why don't they put them closer to the edge and then they would be easier to access?"

Whin shrugged. "I don't know. Perhaps it's so that they stand out and then people can see them from far away."

"I will tell you a little about the farmers and the rural community" Whin continued. "They had a very tough existence until recently. After the war when it was extremely difficult getting the land back to a state that could be cultivated, many needed to migrate to the cities to find work to get money to send back to their families. The government could see that this would lead to inner city problems with an increasing population and a potential increase in unemployment and begging. So now, if they want to build a new factory or encourage outside investment from foreign companies, they encourage the building of such near the rural towns so that farmers can earn a living near their homes. The farmers are generally multi-skilled in farming, building and mechanics, and are strong for general manual work. They can pretty much turn their hand to anything."

"That sounds like a really sensible thing to do." I interjected. "There are so many cities in the world that are becoming sprawling metropolises, because the rural people migrate to the cities, and not only do they not find work but the infrastructure breaks under the back of the population increase. At least here you are taking the work to the people and not the people to the work."

"There are still some companies that want to build manufacturing plants on the outskirts of Hanoi but a lot of medium sized companies go to the country." She replied. "They have a ready and willing workforce and it fosters goodwill in the community." I reckoned that they didn't suffer from NIMBY's in Vietnam.

The Vietnamese overall were a very hardworking people, driven by wanting to rebuild their country, unlike some other Asian countries, where you see hundreds of people just hanging around with nothing much to do. The Vietnamese were extremely proud of their country and hence looked forward to rebuilding it and creating a good life for all rather than dwelling on their invasions of the past.

We arrived in Halong Bay. There was a marina full of lovely old Vietnamese ships and boats, with strong tall masts and beautifully carved decorations. Some were like dragon heads and had been painted also. However, Halong Bay was totally geared up for tourism, but what the hell, it was extremely picturesque all the same.

I had my own boat again of course. The bay was called "Falling Down Dragon Bay" because of the unusual limestone rock formations jutting severely out of the water looked like the tails of dragons. There were about 3000 of these little islands. It was not dissimilar to Guilin in China and felt equally eerie. I hadn't seen the film The Lord of the Rings, but it was the sort of landscape you would imagine hobbits living in. Unfortunately it was a very hazy day so I didn't get to see it at its best.

We arrived and docked at the first island where there were some caves to visit. There were 100 steps to mount to visit the first cave, but I was now used to steps this holiday, given the number of places only accessed by such. The caves were only discovered a few years ago by some fishermen who crept behind the greenery covering the entrance to shelter from a storm, and made the amazing discovery.

The first cave, The Cave of Heaven, was absolutely stunning. It was about the height of a six storey building with remarkable stalagmites and stalactites and other rock formations. The fishermen must have been totally struck down with awe when they discovered it. UNESCO had donated some money to light up the cave and put a walkway through. It was truly, truly stunning and probably the best grotto I'd ever seen. There were some ominous looking cracks in the ceiling so I guessed that sadly one day it will come tumbling down.

The second cave "The cave of wooden spikes" was disappointing by comparison as it was not as well lit up nor as beautiful. It was called the Wooden Spikes cave because it was one of the caves where the wooden stakes were made and stored, for placing in the water to deter enemies.

After the caves, I got back on board my boat for a cruise around the unusual islands, and had lunch. We were served a delicious seafood lunch cooked on the boat whole crab, prawns, spring rolls, grilled fish in ginger, onions and tomatoes, sticky rice, squid and a cabbage like vegetable. It was absolutely delectable..

We passed by house boats anchored above their fishing patches. I was told that the boat people lived on their boats and even had a floating school for the kids. It was a very tranquil cruise and agreeable way to spend some time.

Sadly, all too soon it was time to go back to land and take the return journey to Hanoi. Surprise surprise though, on the way back to the shore out came the handicrafts to buy. However, the woman was really sweet and not at all pushy, almost as if she were a little embarrassed to be trying to make a sale, so I bought a pearl necklace (fresh water pearls) for ten dollars and a packet of post cards that showed what Halong Bay looked like when it wasn't hazy. They were all so cheap that I bought loads of extra ones just to be able to give more money without insulting her by making it look like a charity donation. She probably had no respect for me anyway because I didn't bargain, but as everything was so cheap by Western standards, I just couldn't bring myself to bargain at all on this occasion.

On the way back to Hanoi, Whin told me some of the war horror stories, partially provoked by me asking her how the Vietnamese could possibly welcome the French and Americans to their country considering the devastation they had both caused, especially the Americans as that war was only one generation ago, and there would still be many with memories of that era. I had learned throughout the holiday that the Vietnamese look forward, not backward, and therefore Americans were generally welcomed. The French destroyed everything as they left. We drove past a power station which was built by the French but as they left, they totally wrecked it beyond use. It was only thanks to investment from the Japanese and Australians that they were able to rebuild it and get it working again. The French did the same to most of the factories and bridges they had built. Such spite.

She also told me about the Son My Massacre in the hamlets of My Lai and My Khe, where around five hundred unarmed civilians were raped, tortured and murdered by the United States Army soldiers of "Charlie" Company in 1968, The victims included women, men, children, and infants. Some of the women were gang-raped prior to being murdered. Initially twenty six soldiers were charged with the atrocities, but only one was convicted. Found guilty of killing twenty two villagers, he was originally given a life sentence, but only served three and a half years under house arrest. The massacre didn't become public knowledge until 1969 which subsequently increased domestic opposition in the U.S.A to involvement in the Vietnam War.

Three U.S. servicemen who had tried to halt the massacre and protect the wounded were initially denounced as traitors and received hate mail and death threats. However they were later praised for their actions, exonerated and decorated. There was another village nearby where the Americans killed all the men and old people and repeatedly raped the women over several days, many of whom fell pregnant with GI kids. After the war, a group of the soldiers who had committed these atrocities returned to the village and apparently fell to their knees and wept and wept when they saw what they had left behind, women having to do all their dead men's work, and their children growing up in abject poverty, some shunned because they looked more American than Vietnamese.

Many of the American kids born in Vietnam during the war were expatriated to the USA. They were colloquially known as Bui Doi in modern culture, following the success of the musical Miss Saigon, although the term actually means "less than dust" and was originally used within Vietnam as a degrading word for vagrants and starving people of the countryside taking refuge in towns.

Initially post war the USA did little to help rebuild Vietnam despite promising funding, although in recent years they had now started investing in factories and commercial enterprises. However, even this was controversial as some Vietnamese believed it was not "aid" disguised as investment because of past wrong doings, but exploitation of cheap labour.

The only people to be apparently more vicious to the Vietnamese than the Americans, were the South Koreans. They slowly tortured their victims to death, cutting off parts of their body a bit at a time. Hand, foot, nose, ear, tongue, breasts, penis.

It was starting to get dark outside and driving was becoming more hazardous. I thought that if I lived in Vietnam for the rest of my life I would never work out their driving system. Generally it seemed that the bigger you were, the greater your right of way. However, there was also a code of beeping and flashing which meant either "get out of the way I'm coming through" or "you can go first" or " I'm here – avoid me" or "thanks for letting me through", but I'll be damned if I could ever work out which was which.

I asked Whin if she had a car.

"Oh no, very expensive. Plus there is a government rule saying that you can't own a car unless you have a garage to be able to keep it off the road. This vastly reduces the number of vehicles on the road as most people have flats or terraced houses with no such facilities." I guessed the same applied to motorbikes, which was why Jin and his brothers had stored theirs in his living room.

I noticed that Whin didn't wear a wedding ring, but then I wasn't certain whether that was the same symbol as back home, so I asked her,

"Are you married Whin?" She laughed and then said, "No, I still live with my parents and grandparents. I live in the old part of the city near the market we visited yesterday. Once you are married here, you are expected to look after the rest of the family and extended family. If I got married, my husband would move in to my house and I would be expected to cook, clean etc for the whole family. That would be the end of my career."

"But couldn't you look after the home and have a career?" I quizzed

"No, it would be frowned upon. In any case I wouldn't have enough hours in the day! Things are changing here. The younger generation are putting off marriage as long as possible. They have a sense of freedom now because of education and there are many careers open to them."

She told me that she was twenty six and wouldn't consider marriage until at least twenty eight, probably later, as she enjoyed her career and was not ready yet to swap it for housekeeping.

Back at the hotel, I felt pretty exhausted simply because of the distance up to Halong Bay and back again and I decided to try the e-mail again which worked that night. There was an E-mail from Joe telling me not to worry about him. He was back on speaking terms with Penny although it sounded like the "spark" had temporarily gone. It was a shame he hadn't the courage to have a go at being on his own. Yes, the path was paved with broken glass, invisible objects to trip you up and holes to fall into, but at the other end, there was most definitely a green field. I have known several men and a few women who just can't cope with not having a partner, and move to the next relationship with alarming alacrity regardless of suitability, because the option of being alone is just too scary. I think that is so sad.

There was also a message from Stephen obviously trying to wind me up as he said that I have probably eaten loads of dog without knowing it and that I'm due a guilt trip. Good job I was used to his sense of humour.

I wasn't hungry that evening which was hardly surprising after the fantastic lunch, so I just had a Tiger Beer liquid dinner and brought the diary up to date.

There was obviously a wedding or something going on in the hotel, as there were loads of kids running up and down the escalators the wrong way screaming and screeching, with parents who were either oblivious, or just didn't give a damn. I retired to my room.

Hanoi - 30th December

It was my last full day in Vietnam and I had designated it as a "day at leisure". What should I do? There was nowhere around the hotel to sit in comfort as even the pool was under cover, so it was going to be a walking tour of Hanoi city. The aim was to see a little more than I did in the whirlwind tour of a couple of days ago. I also wanted to try and see the Water Puppets show that I'd heard so much about, so decided to see if I could get a ticket for that at short notice. I could look to see if there were any jewellery shops where I might find a ring and I also wanted to buy a bottle of snake wine. I saw loads of these in the south but hadn't seen any since. What was I saying a few days back about buying things when you had the opportunity to?

I walked along the banks of Swan Lake, down past the tower with the Vietnamese flag and saw Uncle Ho's mausoleum looming in the distance.

After walking for about an hour, I stumbled across the one and only department store in Hanoi. It was air-conditioned and quiet, so I decided to give it a try. It was pretty much like any other department store in the world, except that everything was jumbled up. You just found, for example, the ladies clothes floor, and lo and behold, there was also a tourist gift area in amongst the clothes. I came across the jewellery area, which was pretty large, and looked for a ring. Part of me told me that I'd be paying over the odds here, compared with "Silver Street" in the old quarter for example, but on the other hand, I was more likely to get the genuine article and not a piece of tin. Not being a jewellery connoisseur in the least, I wouldn't be able to tell the difference between a ruby and a piece of coloured glass, so I had to buy from reputable places as I lacked the personal knowledge.

I found two rings that were appealing and selected the one made half from yellow gold and half from white gold. There were two teeny weeny diamonds in it. The ring was too small even to fit my little finger, but the girl told me that she could have it enlarged in an hour. I noticed that Besame Mucho was playing on the shops piped music system. It was one of my favourite accordion and jazz pieces and so being a positive omen, I purchased this ring for circa one hundred pounds and went off to stroll for an hour while it was being adjusted.

Not far from the department store I found a little grassed area off the main road, where I had a rest, and mulled over the holiday.

A young crippled man came up to me in a buggy. He was missing both his legs from above the knees. He was ever so polite as he asked me if I wanted to buy any postcards, unlike the average hawker who was not just under your nose, but halfway up it as well. I didn't really want any as it was the end of the holiday, but perhaps this guy was a child of Agent Orange or a victim of an unexploded bomb, so I picked a pack of post cards and give him 50,000 Dong which was about two pounds. He said that they were only 10,000 Dong and did I want another batch? I said no, and gesticulated for him to keep the rest of the money. I suddenly had an idea and asked him if he wanted some pens, thinking that he could sell these along with the post cards to make a little extra money. He nodded, so I took out my remaining biros, about fifty of them wrapped in a

122

shower cap, and gave them to him. His face beamed back at me. "Thank you, thank you, thank you," he kept saying. He thrust another packet of postcards into my hands and said, "Gift." I thanked him, and he thanked me again before wheeling off into the distance.

I returned to the jewellers and collected the ring. No, I didn't need the box as I was going to wear it right then. It was for my middle finger right hand and it felt strange. It was a long time since I had worn a ring of any description. This was my gift to myself for future positive thinking.

I headed down to the Water Puppet Theatre to book a ticket. I was fortunate that there was only one show that day at 2.30pm. Usually there were two in the evening, but an afternoon matinee meant that I didn't have to go all the way back to the hotel to go out again. It was 1.00pm, so I found a restaurant overlooking Turtle Lake where I ordered a plate of shrimp noodle. There was a choice of a small or large portion, and on the assumption that "small" meant starters and "large" meant main course, I ordered a large portion. What of course the menu should have said was "main course" and "banquet sized" portions, so I was faced with a colossal plate of fried noodles – delicious.

After lunch I went and watched the Water Puppet show. Each puppet was moved around by a stick under water, the puppeteers behind the back drop standing in the water. They were incredibly clever and effective. There were about 10 different scenes, each depicting either a famous legend or showing local rural life. The show was about an hour long and extremely impressive. It couldn't be much fun for the puppeteers being up to their waists in water behind the scene, but I was so glad that I went to see them as it was a very unusual art and I was unlikely to see anything like this again.

I went back to the hotel via the old quarter, keeping half an eye open for some snake wine. I was told in the south that the locals do actually drink it as a "cure all" so it was not simply a tourist gimmick. The bottles came with little labels explaining in English the benefits of taking a glass each day to cure rheumatism, lumbago, strains, depression, premature ejaculation, fertility problems, prevention of the onset of senility, to name just a few. I did come across a shop that sold snake wine, but the bottles didn't have the same labels as those in the south, so part of the "joke" was missing.

The old quarter was as bustling as it was the other day, and I weaved in and out the narrow streets feeling pretty confident that I knew where I was going, until I reached Flower Street, which was where I had started.....

The Vietnamese seemed to eat all the time. I passed a group of 6 or 7 sitting on the pavement tucking into a large pan of duck and noodles. They sat on the tiniest of stools, which I swear I'd have been lucky to get one cheek on. There were food vendors everywhere, whether it was a hot food stand, or a wandering lady with trays of fruit and sweets. I bought a stick of mini donuts from one of them and they were very tasty. I was sure their eating habits were "little and often" rather than two square meals a day. I have a great love of food and enjoy trying foods I haven't eaten before. There are very few things I don't like and I always say that I will try something at least once. I remembered seeing Gone with the Wind

124

as a young child, and the section before the interval where Scarlett O'Hara falls to her knees at Tara and swears that "As god was my witness I'll never go hungry again". It must had had a huge impact on me, because whenever I'm travelling, for holiday or business, I eat at every opportunity because I don't know when I'll get my next meal. Perhaps the Vietnamese developed a similar mentality post war? However, as many didn't have refrigeration in their homes, they shopped for fresh food at least twice a day, so this would impact their eating habits as well.

I was lost at Flower Street, so it was time to use my one dollar map. It was not the simplest of maps to follow with all the streets names being long and complicated Vietnamese words, but I managed to pin point my location and eventually found my way back to the hotel. Some "day at leisure" as I'd walked my little socks off so of course a couple of well deserved Tiger beers were required. Considering that at home I was virtually tea-total, it had just dawned on me how many times in the last 10 days or so I had written "Tiger beers" in the diary.

I set out for my last meal in Vietnam, and chose a local restaurant in the open air, full of young locals. It was by the side of Swan Lake. I choose crab soup, two fresh crabs and a plate of fried prawns in garlic. I noticed that the menu included swan, and I was tempted to try it, but imagined it would be as greasy as goose. The menu also included "fried frog skin" and "stuffed fish stomach". There was a selection of wild boar dishes, which was probably a synonym for "dog", so I avoided these. There was also a selection of rabbit dishes, which was probably a synonym for "little dog" as I hadn't seen any evidence of rabbits during the holiday, so I avoided these too. Although I enjoyed trying new foods, I decided that it was best to play safe and stick to tried and tested seafood as I had a long journey home the next day and didn't want to risk any adverse reactions on a long flight. I was slightly disconcerted when a large rat scurried by the leg of my table, but as they say, when in Rome....

The meal cost about six pounds and that included my beer. I finished and went back to the hotel for my last night in Hanoi.

Homeward bound - 31st December

It was the last day, and I tipped everything out of the day bag and the suitcase I'd effectively lived out of for the past two weeks onto the bed, keeping my fingers crossed that everything would fit back in again. I'd had years of practice and considered that I had an art in packing up post holiday suitcases, so that I didn't have to go through customs with the *"very obvious recently purchased additional suitcase to bring back the booty"* in tow. I really can fit a quart into a pint, and amazingly everything went in with ease, although I had discarded a few books along the way.

My pick up was at 12.00 noon and it was half an hour to the airport.

En-route I asked Whin about the Vietnamese eating habits after my observations the day before, and she told me that they view food solely as fuel, so had lots of little snacks to keep them going throughout the day. They eat to live, and didn't live to eat.

We arrived at the airport and Whin insisted on seeing me through the various check in places. She told me that her duty was not over until I went through to departures. Thank goodness again for air miles and business class, as the queue for economy was out of sight. Whin was a little taken aback that I was travelling business class so I explained about the "use them or lose them" air miles I had accumulated. Check in was pretty painless, but somewhat irritating that I had to pay two hundred and ten thousand Dong foreign exit tax, which was nothing more than a ploy to get more money out of tourists. Luckily Whin had warned me yesterday about this, so I'd kept some money back as they only took cash. I bid farewell and headed to departures. I had about an hour and a half to wait for the flight.

I browsed the duty free. Cigarettes and booze were cheaper on the Malaysian airlines flight from Kuala Lumpur, so I'd wait until then. I didn't normally use my alcohol allowance, however I wanted to take my neighbours Stuart and Mary a bottle of something as a thank you for keeping an eye on my house.

I had a few hundred thousand dong left, which still made me feel like a millionaire even though it was somewhere in the region of fifteen pounds. You couldn't change the money outside of the country so I might as well try and spend it. I considered buying some perfume, but that was quite expensive. I then noticed a small local gifts shop, and they sold snake wine – yes! However, the bottles containing the snakes didn't have the labels, and the wine with the labels didn't have an actual snake in them. So I got a bottle of each, and still had money left to spend. You just couldn't get rid of these Dong.

Three hours to Kuala Lumpur, then a five hour wait for the final flight home. Not a big problem because Kuala Lumpur has one of the best airports in the world and certainly the most comfortable executive lounge I'd ever used. Large, spacious and clean, with food to eat, drinks to drink, free internet access, television and showers. I showed incredible will power and didn't dive into the food, as I knew I'd get a large meal on the plane. I also don't drink

128

alcohol when flying, so limited myself to an orange juice and an aspirin, to counteract any DVT potential.

There was of course an irony here. The 11.45pm, 31st December, Kuala Lumpur flight back to the UK was the exact same flight I'd taken after the holiday in hell with Joe, which led to us splitting up as partners, though as you will have read and realised, we retained a great friendship. But the chances of getting the same flight from such a distant place must be quite remote. It certainly hadn't been planned that way.

I sank into the inviting arm chair and reflected on the holiday

I had been very taken by the country and the people. They were genuinely optimistic, happy, welcoming, friendly and hard working. I felt safer walking the streets of Saigon and Hanoi at night than I did in Aylesbury.

Their last war with the USA had totally, utterly devastated and destroyed their country, but they were working so very hard to rebuild it, and also looking to the future and not dwelling on the past. I had seen and heard a very different side to that portrayed by your typical American "Nam" movie. OK, I'm a realist and as an intelligent woman, I know I would have been fed a large dose of propaganda, but even striping that away, there was clearly a side I wasn't aware of before going there, and there are always at least two sides to every story.

I had loved Saigon with its tremendous atmosphere, superb architecture and lots of interesting places to visit. The War Remnants museum had been distressing, shocking and emotional but a must for any visit. The Cu Chi tunnels used by the Viet Cong had been one of the many highlights of the holiday, especially after understanding more about their construction and ingenious methods of surviving underground.

The Mekong Delta was simply beautiful - peaceful with oodles of ambience, and the Floating Market was an incredible experience. Can Tho was a lovely unspoiled town to walk around and take in the Vietnamese culture but Hoi An on the other hand, although being a lovely restored old typical Vietnamese town with oodles of ambience, was unfortunately a little "touristy". Hue town wasn't anything special but the old dynasty tombs surrounding it were fascinating.

Hanoi had many interesting historical sites, including Uncle Ho's embalmed body. The Water Puppet show had been a unique experience and the many lakes and gardens in the city gave it an open feeling. The old quarter had been brilliant to walk through although I had been pestered the most by hawkers in Hanoi.

I had been unlucky with the foggy weather in Halong Bay but it hadn't detracted from an excellent trip for the unusually shaped mountains jutting out from the sea.

The food throughout the holiday was nothing short of stunning in both display and flavours, and I was 99% certain that I hadn't eaten dog. I had been a little disappointed with a few of the hotels that were just large and impersonal, but then that was my fault for not checking the proposed itinerary before booking. It would be something I'd look out for with my next holiday.

I had been fortunate to have three excellent guides who spoke very good English and were extremely knowledgeable, each taking me on little excursions off the beaten paths.

Most importantly though, I had been alone all holiday, even though I'd initially expected to be joining a group, and with hindsight I had much preferred this. Tour guides took me off the main trail, so I saw and learned much more than the average tourist. Indeed, when I saw some tourist groups I thanked my lucky stars that I was alone. I had my own car, and even on the boat trips, my own boat. I ate all my meals alone yet I didn't suffer any loneliness, experienced a lot of happiness and tranquillity having had only one very minor "wobble" in Hanoi. Out of choice I would never join a group holiday again, unless it couldn't be avoided.

The holiday was expensive, but worth every penny. It wasn't a "holiday" as most people think of "holidays", but I had the most wonderful, truly enjoyable and exhilarating experience and it is up there with the "best ever" holidays.

The flight back was awful only because I was tired and wanted to sleep but there was a baby screaming and squealing a couple of seats away from me and the parents were doing absolutely nothing to stop it. A little like the parents in Supermarkets who think their kid is "cute" if it's bawling its head off and running amok. I mused about the potential of putting babies and misbehaving children in the hold with the luggage. I complained to the flight attendant that I didn't travel business class not to get any sleep. She unsympathetically offered me earplugs.

I picked up the in-flight magazine and turned to the world map. It looked so small stretched over just two pages. Where should I travel to next? A new continent I thought, yes, South America.......

Other books in the Travelling Solo series

Brazil and Argentina: From Jungle to Icebergs
The Gambia: Land of the Mandinka

If you want to know more about the author and future writing plans, please visit:

www.susanrogersauthor.co.uk

Thank you.